CITY. STORY. US.

A Journey of Resistance, Hope, and Surrender

Susan G. Spousta

Urban Loft Publishers | Skyforest, CA

CITY. STORY. US.
A Journey of Resistance, Hope, and Surrender

Urban Loft Publishers
P.O. Box 6
Skyforest, CA 92385
www.urbanloftpublishers.com

Senior Editors: Stephen Burris & Kendi Howells Douglas
Copy Editor: Marla Black
Graphics: Brittnay Parsons
Cover Design: Elizabeth Arnold

Unless otherwise noted, Scripture quotations are taken from the *Holy Bible*, New Living Translation, copyright © 1996, 2004, 2015 by Tyndale House Foundation. Used by permission of Tyndale House Publishers, Inc., Carol Stream, Illinois 60188. All rights reserved.

ISBN-13: 978-1-949625-12-7

Made in the U.S

Praise for *City. Story. Us.*

"Spousta excels at chronicling her own honest and revealing journey of discovering a call to the city and integrating it with the best thinking on urban transformation. In the process she provides accessible onramps for others to join in the journey."

> -Dr. Randy White, Director, FPU Center for Community Transformation and Author of *Out of Nazareth: Christ-Centered Civic Transformation in Unlikely Places*

"Sue Spousta's City. Story.Us. is a treasure-trove of missional, theological, and practical insight from someone who has actually done it. It seems almost insane that the idea of a Christian going to the city in love has been reversed by a church that has fled to the burbs. But this has happened. And voices like Sue's are a clarion call back to our original mission—to be blessed that we might bless the whole world. Even the city! A must read for any who hear God's call to love the urban world."

> -Dr. A. J. Swoboda, Assistant Professor of Bible and Theology at Bushnell University and author of *After Doubt* (Brazos).

"Susan has given us a well-researched book on the beauty and tragedy of the modern city. As someone who lives in and loves the city, I was immediately hooked. What I was unprepared for was the intimate story of how God uses the city as a pallet to endlessly surprise us – blending grit, glamour, and heartache to reshape the future. Susan offers us, not only the fact of the city, but the metaphor of the city as a transforming and redemptive instrument of grace."

> -Sam Rockwell, PhD, Supervisor, Gateway District Foursquare Churches

*"Sue Spousta's love for cities, the Church, and the Good News oozes from every page of **City. Story. Us.** At a time where we may be tempted toward safety and retreat, she calls us to eagerly seek the shalom of the cities to which God has called us. To see the beauty as well as the challenge of the city as a call to deeper intimacy with Christ, who is there already. To be captivated by the joy of the Good News lived and shared, proclaimed and demonstrated in lives of action and justice. We need our cities, and our cities need us."*

-Kevin Palau, President, Luis Palau Association

"Well-researched, fluidly written, expertly crafted - Sue Spousta's CITY. STORY. US is a powerful work which weaves together personal anecdote, biblical principle, and theological paradigm into a beautiful resource for those called to make their home in cities. As one who began a church in New York City three and a half years ago, I found myself nodding in agreement at the missiological convictions and theological balance put forth in this book. Simply put - a must read."

-Russell Joyce, Senior Pastor, Hope Church, Brooklyn, NY

"In CITY. STORY. US., Sue Spousta beautifully and plainly shares stories that are both challenging and inspiring. You can't help but be swept along with her. She moves us from gentle theological reflection on our own incomplete Gospel and personal resistance, to finding a hope and beauty in the practical choices before us. By the end of the book you will feel compelled that the renewal of our hearts is incomplete until we see that same Jesus-renewal reflected in the faces in our neighborhoods and communities around us."

-Jessie Cruickshank, 100 Movements Ecosystem Lead Driver and 5Q Co-founder

"James K. A. Smith, in, <u>Desiring the Kingdom</u>, argues that if we aim only for the head, we will capture neither the heart nor the mind. However, if

we aim for the heart we will change both heart and mind. Sue Spousta changes the reader's understanding of the city, by drawing us into her heart for the city and then leading us to practical wisdom and sound theology."

-Sam Winston, Regional Overseer for the Middle East, North Africa and Central Asia for Foursquare Missions International

"At a time when many of us are awakening to the importance of bridging economic, racial, and social divides, Spousta's engaging, informative narrative journey of discovery, resistance, and hope toward loving her city can help us identify and more fully participate in our own. Smartly laid out and beautifully written, the book also helpfully includes the interesting journeys and lessons of several other 'urban practitioners.'"

-Steve Overman, Lead Pastor, Eugene Faith Center and adjunct professor, Portland Seminary at George Fox University

"We recommend this book to any Christian weary of the status quo and hungry for an authentic life filled with kingdom adventure and challenge. Susan Spousta is like the mother eagle who rips apart the soft nesting her eaglets had been resting in so they might be taught to fly and fulfill the purpose for which they were created. She is admittedly, "a servant of God messed over by the Holy Spirit," and she invites us into this messed over state with her. This book is raw, humorous, engaging, and challenging; written by a woman who is vulnerable, courageous and one who has allowed her fears to be turned into hope. Only the brave will make it through this read; those willing to resist their own "nesting" of comfort, surrender their fears, and embrace the risk to become hope for the broken. Simply said, this book feels like Jesus."

-Art and Sharon Snow, Co-pastors, Chestnut Street Community Church, Roselle, N.J.
Administrator, Chestnut Street Learning Center

"*CITY. STORY. US. is a book of love and conviction, prompting us to reach beyond our comfort zones and freely give the Savior's hope to those we thought unreachable. Filled with practical, personal stories Sue challenges city fears and encourages us to fully live for Christ, whatever our calling and wherever our city.*"

> -Cathe Wiese, Founder and Executive Director, My Father's House Community Shelter

"*City. Story. Us. isn't just a book, it's an autobiographical missional adventure. This book is weighted, hopeful, and accessible, because Sue carries the weight of experience, a hopeful imagination, and an accessible outlook of the church and all that she can be in this decade. Read this book, or even better, let it read you.*"

> -Greg Russinger, Pastor, Alongsiders Church and Co-founder, Laundry Love

"*Sue Spousta's ministry is a rich tapestry of experience, insight, and sensitivity to the work of God in the world. City. Story. Us. captures her heart for God's vision for creating holy communities. Spousta's honesty, wisdom, and many practical insights will encourage and inspire readers with hope for the "right and righteous path" of God.*"

> -Leah Payne, PhD, Associate Professor of Theology, Portland Seminary

"*Susan presents the Good News, not as a 'project' or 'activity' for our cities, but as the integration of mission in our daily lives. Readers will identify with the author's journey as a challenge for the Church to draw close to the heart of God and neighbor. CITY. STORY. US. is honest, compelling, and filled with hope. Highly recommended!*"

> -Dr. Gea Gort, Business as Mission Initiator, the Netherlands; author of *God in the City: A Missional Way of Life in an Urban*

Context and *BAM Global Movement: Business as Mission Concept and Stories*

Dedicated to . . .

My husband, Larry, for his tireless support, encouragement, and unconditional love.

My son, Matt, whose love for reading and intrinsic value for lifelong learning prompted his mother to re-enter the land of higher education.

My daughter, Stacey, who meets each day with such delight in others, I cannot help but smile at God as he delights in her.

My grandchildren who, without a doubt, will be God's transformational agents in the cities to which God calls them.

Special thanks to . . .

Urban pastor, Greg Russinger, for his insightful view of city ministry and spiritual practices that connect God, community, and church.

The Portland area pastors and urban practitioners who helped create and conduct the City. Story. Us. Conference and inspired the title for this book.

Professor of Urban Immersion, Dr. Randy White, for "offending" me with the city so I could love the city with God's heart.

Vice President of Foursquare Operations, Tammy Dunahoo, for encouraging the development of Affinity Networks as a resource to the non-profit leaders of our organization.

Foursquare Affinity Networks, whose participants' experience, expertise, and knowledge of social issues have broadened my mind, engaged my heart, and sent me on a wild journey of discovery.

Lynn Sawyer, Dennis Easter, Phil Newell, and Stephen Burris for their encouragement to write well.

Table of Contents

A Word to Begin 15

Introduction: Truth and the "Lily" 17

Part 1: Resistance 21

    1.   Resisting the Dark Side of Comfort

        Fear and the Status Quo 23

    2.   Resisting an Edited Gospel

        Kingdom and the City 33

    3.   Resisting Injustice

        Mission and Shalom 43

    4.   Resisting Systemic Sin

        History and the Spiritual Battle

        55

Part 2: Hope 67

    5.   Hope For The City

        Finding the Good 69

    6.   Hope For The Least

        Finding Heart 79

7. Hope For The Last
    Finding Innocence 93

8. Hope For The Lost
    Finding Joy 105

9. Hope For The Church
    Finding Center 119

Part 3: Surrender 133

10. Risky Dreams
    Street Surrender 135

11. Risky Business
    Incarnational Surrender 159

12. Risky Rescue
    A Just Surrender, Part A 181

13. Risky Rescue
    A Just Surrender, Part B 199

Conclusion: The Story Continues With Us 215

A Final Word 219

References 223

A Word to Begin

Writing a book that addresses a personal journey can leave the reader with the impression that the author has gone somewhere and subsequently arrived at his destination *or* is going somewhere with an endpoint she has not yet reached. I pray that this account unfolds a story of both realities. Inexperience, weighted and balanced by an awakened soul, has set me on a journey that is temporal and eternal, personal and collective. It has been realized in the straight path of uncompromised faith and equally in the ever-twisting, circuitous road of shared experiences that continue to stretch my theology and enlarge my heart.

My journey and the timing of this book have been God-ordained. As with all my life-destinations, I arrived at authorship much in the same way I arrived at marriage, parenthood, ministry, and education . . . surprised and, well . . . feeling unprepared. Either too early or too late has been the story of my life. I got married *too* young. I earned my degree *too* late in life (at least by usual standards!). Honestly, what I can say is that God has always been on time.

In light of my journey, the pages that follow are not about an accomplished urban practitioner, but rather a servant of God "messed over" by the Holy Spirit. I don't presume to create a new missional theology, set the Church on a wildly innovative trajectory toward urban transformation, or wow brilliant theological minds. I expect to present my personal struggle, a resistance to what I did not know, and the glorious resurgence of hope I've discovered for myself as a Christ-follower and for His precious Bride, the Church. This is a past, present, and future journey that I pray will resonate and encourage others toward an urban change-of-heart. May past perceptions give way to God's unbridled movement in the cities of our world. May we continue to "go somewhere" together, regardless of where we have been.

Introduction

Truth and the "Lily"

"Take me by the hand;
Lead me down the path of truth.
You are my Savior, aren't you?
From now on every road you travel will take you to God.
Follow the Covenant signs;
Read the charted directions."
Psalm 25:5, 10 (The Message)

Recently, on the eve of a final vacation day, my husband and I curled up on the sofa to watch a movie. *CONCUSSION* had long since played in theatres but was available via our cable company's "On Demand" feature. When the movie was first released the trailer intrigued us, so we clicked "PLAY MOVIE" and settled in for some free and interesting entertainment.

CONCUSSION is based on the true story of Dr. Bennet Omalu, a coroner who discovered Chronic Traumatic Encephalopathy (CTE) after examining the corpse of Pittsburg Steeler's player, Mike Webster. The movie highlights the dangers of repeated concussive blows and their connection to CTE, a condition that causes severe mental illness and dementia. Omalu's research, as one might imagine, was not well received by the National Football League. At the height of the doctor's efforts to bring awareness to the tremendous risks players were taking, the persecution from fans, the

NFL, and some colleagues became almost unbearable. At this low point, Bennet, an immigrant to the U.S. from Nigeria, describes to his wife, Prema, the reason he came to America: "I came to America because I thought here you could do anything, *be* anything. Americans were the manifestation of what God wanted all of us to be." Then he quickly expresses his frustration and disillusionment: "But Mike Webster goes mad and nobody asks why. They make fun of him. And now they want to pretend this disease doesn't exist? They want to bury me? It's offensive. I'm offended. I'm the wrong person to have discovered this."[1] Prema responds with a clarity and confidence:

> There is no coincidence in this world. Tell me. What is the statistical probability that you, not just a doctor, but Bennet Omalu, came to America, end up here, this rusty place, for you alone to be the one to see this? When I arrived in New York, I was attacked . . . that man almost broke me. I wanted to give up and go back. But I knew God; I decided to trust his wisdom. And now I am looking at *this* man, an Omalu Onyemalukube. Your name. It means, if you know, you must come forth and speak . . . If you don't speak for the dead, who will?[2]

The inspiration of Prema's words runs deep. Bennet's journey, despite the opposition, was God-directed not coincidental. He had been chosen to *see* and *speak*—to tell the truth because he knew the truth.

Over the last several years, I've seen a very different view of the gospel than the one I've observed through the symbiotic eyes of denominational tradition and evangelicalism. Gaining a more holistic discovery of salvation, deliverance, and justice has confronted my soul and imagination with the possibilities of God's kingdom on earth as it is in

---

[1] SCRIPTS, "Concussion," https://www.scripts.com/script-pdf/304, 2016, accessed (December 4, 2016). 69.
[2] Ibid. 70.

heaven. It has, at the very same time, garnered resistance and exposed the complacent, often self-righteousness, sometimes all-knowing person I can be. Like the NFL, I would rather *not* know, choosing to believe things are fine as they are and accept no responsibility for the eventual outcomes. Like the fans, I would rather believe people *go* nuts than understand the cause of the craziness. And, even after facing my own blindness and complacency, not unlike Dr. Omalu, I often feel I was the wrong person to be entrusted with this wild idea that believers can do something about the repeated societal concussions taking place in our world. It all boils down to, if I know, I have to speak and act (even though my name literally means "a lily of the valley!"), listening well to the lessons of those who have suffered or are suffering and allowing them to once again discover their own voice.

Whenever the temptation arises to wish I'd never encountered poverty, been exposed to the suffering of trafficked human beings, watched racial injustice rear its ugly head, felt the pain of a refugee trying to begin a new life; I remember God, in His wisdom, orchestrated this discovery for me and for his Church. His life exemplified the courage to love humanity in its present state of "chronic trauma." It was just as natural for him to touch a person with a contagious disease, accept a sip of water from a prostitute, or dine with a crooked politician as it was to hang with his best friends or go to synagogue. He rubbed shoulders with humanity to bring them a tangible hope that would one day culminate in a new reality of reconciliation with their Maker and with one another: peace, health, love, abundance and joy beyond belief!

In the face of this unprecedented hope, Scripture is not easy on us, his Church. We must love as Christ loved—all the way to the margins. That is risky. Embracing those who are "other" and "different" offends our sensibilities. Neither is it easy to challenge long held theological moorings, consumer-oriented Western church values, or Christian cultural milieus that keep believers, like me, neatly distanced from real-world pain and suffering. Space and proximity to the present need have become increasingly important to combat Christian insulation. The highly edited version of the gospel, once unchallenged, now drives me to take God's hand and let him "lead me down the path of Truth." My prayer is that my journey, every road I travel, will begin and end in Him as I follow the "Covenant signs" and read the "charted directions." There is a purpose and a God-directed journey that is far from coincidental—*even* for a delicate lily!

Coincidences turned divine providence when I was introduced to a graduate program with the city as its focus. Bakke Graduate University served as a directional change, opening my world to urban issues and the city itself as key components of the mission of God. This book contains many of the lessons I *experienced* (saw, heard, touched, and lived) while completing a degree in Urban Leadership. As with all worthy academic endeavors, these lessons pave the path of application and participation that lasts a lifetime. For this reason, I've chosen to divide the book into three parts. Part One, *RESISTANCE,* will describe resistance in personal, systemic, and historical terms. Part Two, *HOPE*, will connect God's functional, present hope for places and people while informing the motivations that build for God's Kingdom. Finally, Part Three, *SURRENDER,* will open the imagination to a future generation of leaders that love their cities with a Christ-empowered creativity, relevancy, and fruitfulness.

Our journey is not coincidental. The CITY has a STORY intricately woven in the gospel narrative, a story in progress and, quite remarkably, one that includes you and me—all of US moving forward, learning, living, and sharing Truth.

Part 1

Resistance

City-apprehension is diminished as we understand God's plan and mission. As our minds are renovated by the Spirit, our hearts are transformed. Life changes in the best possible way. Personal resistance softens, while resistance to anything other than a whole Gospel becomes radically resolute.

1

Resisting the Dark Side of Comfort: Fear and the Status Quo

One night the Lord spoke to Paul in a vision: "Do not be afraid; keep on speaking, do not be silent. For I am with you, and no one is going to attack and harm you, because I have many people in this city.

Acts 18:9,10

In the face of death, live humanly. In the middle of chaos, celebrate the Word . . . And more than that, in the Word of God . . . raise those who are dead in mind and in conscience.

~ William Stringfellow, *An Ethic for Christians and Other Aliens in a Strange Land*

There is nothing wrong with a desire for safety or the comfort of belonging—that wonderful feeling that begs to soothe human fears with the knowledge that *I belong here among people that are like me.* Safe place. Safe people. Almost anyone who has experienced a close call in an urban or inner city context, whether at home or abroad, understands the relief that comes with the realization you are, indeed, physically and emotionally intact. However, if that close call initiates unreasonable, paralyzing fear, safety literally becomes an avoidance of reality.

Reality, as we know, is a mixed bag. We live in a world full of light and darkness, joy and pain, life and death. Often the bad outweighs the good, fostering self-protection and survival while, at the same time, accommodating a passive indifference to the suffering and injustice around us. The tension of what should be and what is becomes very real for individuals and for the church.

William Stringfellow, a lesser-known and somewhat controversial theologian, confronted the internal and external conflict created by the good and evil of a city. Authors Saunders and Campbell highlight Stringfellow's works in their book *Word on the Street: Performing the Scriptures in the Urban Context.* The co-authors explain how Stringfellow, an attorney turned street preacher, used Scripture as a means to combat, literally resist, the principalities and powers of darkness he encountered in the vintage sixties East Harlem neighborhood where he chose to reside. He could often be found audibly reading the Word as he walked the streets, inviting those he encountered into the warmth of his own sparse apartment. What some considered nonsense, Stringfellow saw as the solution to systemic sin. He insisted that the church, in obedience to the Word, was a "foretaste and forerunner . . . of the reconciled society . . . the image of God's own Kingdom."[3] While working against injustice and corruption and for the peace of his neighborhood, Stringfellow experienced the personal struggle of living with kingdom expectations in a threatening environment. His conclusion: resistance *and* hope characterize the Christian life.[4]

To resist the havoc principalities and powers flail about, we, as Christ-followers, must first deal with our own resistance to get involved. Fear is often the first "resistor-of-choice!" We can so easily succumb to the

---

[3] William Stringfellow quoted in Stanley P. Saunders and Charles L. Campbell, *The Word on the Street: Performing the Scriptures in the Urban Context* (Grand Rapids, MI: Wm B. Eerdmans Pub., 2000) 70.
[4] Ibid.

fear of places and people who differ from us, we hear a resounding shout of "Uncle!" while pinned beneath our opponent: Status quo living. The kind of living that accepts as normative the confinement fear imposes.

Fear's Tattoo

What do I have in common with Henry Ford, Diana Ross, and Rosa Parks? While I drive a car, appreciate the Supremes, and admire Rosa Parks, the connection is to the city of Detroit, otherwise known as "Motown." This is where Henry Ford made affordable assembly line automobiles for the average person. This is where Motown Records signed Diana Ross and the Supremes. This is the city to which the famous civil rights activist, Rosa Parks and her husband relocated when the fallout of the Montgomery Bus Boycott caused them to lose their jobs. Moreover, this is the city where I was born to post-World War II parents.

The fact that my father moved north to find work after the war, positioned our family in a racially charged urban environment. Segregation was not mandated by law but was implicit in the city's culture. The tension and distrust were palpable. Though my parents taught us to respect everyone, regardless of color, the influx of blacks into Detroit's urban core wasn't wholly comfortable for my southern born, below the Mason-Dixon line, Hatfield and McCoy feuding, biscuit and gravy family.

As neighborhoods became increasingly black, white families moved out to the suburbs. Whether the move was racially motivated or simply a step up in living conditions, our family followed the white flight when I was very young. Traveling back into the city to visit the aunts, uncles, and cousins who remained was often met with fear. Once in a great while, there would be the horror story, produced from the overactive imagination of young cousins, recounting an enormous *crazy* man pressing his face against a bedroom window screen or a gang of teens making chase to the "Mom and Pop" store located just down the block. Sleepovers with relatives soon became a curious mix of *delicious* fright and outright trepidation. *What new*

stories of danger and intrigue would I hear? Would I make it back home
safe and sound to my little suburban Cape Cod?

The concept of the city as a fearful place was reinforced years later after my mother remarried and moved my sister, brother, and I to a small town just outside Chicago. In the summer of 1967, my stepfather and mother drove my siblings and me back to Michigan for "visitation" with our dad. As the car approached Detroit in late evening, the riots that had begun days before had left the city in an apocalyptic state. The National Guard lined the overpasses with automatic weapons in hand. Storefront windows were broken. Buildings were still smoldering. People wandered the streets. Faces were angry, lost. It resembled the aftermath of a major war zone. I don't think I can adequately describe my eleven-year-old impressions. I certainly didn't understand the grave injustices that prompted the violence, but I surely could not comprehend that people, black or white, could do such a thing. And I was afraid—very afraid.

My childhood fears were later buried under the reason and sophistication of adulthood, but mysteriously appeared with the help of circumstantial triggers. The memories were stained deep into the soft tissue of my heart. The pain had dissipated, but the tattoo-like fear remained as a signal or road sign that there existed an abidance of trouble just ahead.

Since becoming an intelligent, logical grown-up, I've been lost in several major U.S. cities, including my hometown of Detroit. (Apparently, maturity doesn't prevent one from becoming directionally challenged.) In far less dangerous moments, I've felt the fear of riots and death grasp me by the throat. A dark street corner in Los Angeles, a gathering of homeless men under a bridge in Portland, or an aggressive gas station attendant in the abandoned industrial district of Detroit are the type of surfacing scenarios that reinforce my long-held assumption that the city is a dangerous place to be. Granted, it *can* be a dangerous place.

Facing City Danger

The Apostle Paul, called to reach the Gentile world, visited, lived, or was imprisoned in several cities of the Roman Empire and then known world. While each had its unique cultural, religious, and social context, opposition from a variety of sources seemed a frequent commonality. After the Apostle's experience with the highly intellectual, philosophic, idol-worshipping Athenians, Paul arrived in Corinth to face some stiff hostility. His inclusive heart for the Gentiles did not hinder the effort to persuade fellow Jews with the gospel of Christ. In Corinth, Paul presented the message in the marketplace and in the synagogue. The latter got him in trouble. Not only did the Jews reject his teaching, they became verbally abusive, using ugly language to contentiously argue their views. The situation had escalated to such a degree Paul washed his hands of the whole ugly affair and, in a sense, denounced any responsibility for their salvation or damnation.

What is amazing in this story of evangelism-gone-wrong is the phenomenal success that resulted. "Crispus, the synagogue leader and his entire household believed in the Lord; and many of the Corinthians who heard Paul believed and were baptized (Acts 18:8)." That's AMAZING! More remarkable, and somewhat mystifying, is the vision Paul had one night while in Corinth. The vision, or dream, brought these words of consolation from the Lord: "Don't be afraid. Keep on speaking the truth. Don't let anyone silence you. I am with you. No one can hurt you . . . and, by the way, I have lots and lots of friends in this city!" (Acts 18:9-10 Author's paraphrase)

Modern readers of Acts are made to feel as if they missed some important line in the narrative. Didn't a little peacock of an Apostle just tell off an entire group of feisty Jews, audaciously putting them in their place? Paul seems to have his courage intact, so why would God reassure him there was nothing to fear? Without a precise explanation from Scripture, we can deduct from the context that a handful of past experiences haunted Paul's present perception of his surroundings. The fear inked in previous scenarios—the plot to stone he and Barnabas in Iconium; the beating that found him left-for-dead outside Lystra; the thrashing and imprisonment he and Silas endured in Philippi; the abuse his host suffered at the hands of rioters instigating his own stealthy departure from Thessalonica—no doubt played in his imagination. There was no immediate bodily threat in Corinth to Paul or his companions Aquila, Priscilla, Silas, or Timothy, but fear of such harm loomed large in the Apostle.

It would have been highly foolish for Paul to throw all caution to the wind, especially in light of recent "urban" events. I can't help feeling, however, that God was addressing fears that may have kept the Apostle from seeing God's activity in Corinth and subsequently from staying on "for some time" (Acts 18:18) in the city. Most scholars believe that Paul stayed in the city for at least a couple of years, perhaps longer (Acts 18:11, 18).[5] During his visit, after the Lord spoke so plainly that his servant should not be afraid, the Jews of Corinth made a united attack on Paul dragging him before Gallio, the proconsul or judge. Gallio refused to arbitrate, leaving the Jews to settle the matter. In a strange juxtaposition of targets, the crowd turned on Sosthenes, the synagogue leader, beating him with an unrequited vengeance. A man by the name of Sosthenes is mentioned in Paul's later writings to the Corinthians (I Cor 1:1). Some think he may have been Paul's friend[6], while others reason that this Jewish leader became a believer *because* Paul continued in the city.[7] Regardless, the Apostle's eyes were opened to see God's hand at work. No harm would come to him here and, indeed, the Lord had many people in Corinth. Paul wasn't being asked to ignore potential dangers; he was encouraged to see the city through a different lens, a perspective that supersedes fear—real or imagined.

---

[5] Matthew Henry, *Matthew Henry's Commentary on the Whole Bible*, vol. Volume 6, Acts to Revelation (Peabody, MA: Hendrickson Publishers, 1991). 192.

[6] Ibid. 192.

[7] Word Pictures in the New Testament, Volume III, pg 302

Breaking the Hold of Status Quo Living

Seeing through fear, acknowledging God at work, having faith that He is present to us—even in the city—are keys for victory as we wrestle with present realities. Author Amy Sherman admonishes, "To put it succinctly, we need to remember that the kingdom of God is both *now* and *not yet*."[8] To stand firm in the *now* is to believe that Jesus established His kingdom on earth through the incarnation; that he continues to manifest His kingdom through the Church as a result of his death, resurrection, and ascension; and that one day a new heaven and new earth will culminate in a new city. Unfortunately, it is the latter unseen climax of the *not yet* that often prompts the human response to run and hide while masking the retreat as a godly alternative.

The "city fears" I faced early in life led to a decades-long retreat of which I was unaware. After the initial move from urban Detroit, I remained, other than an occasional foray, estranged from the city and blissfully ignorant of its woes—and its joys. From an economic and security viewpoint, society reinforced suburban living as ideal, while the church, seemingly to me, touted places outside urban centers as tranquil sanctuaries for Christians living the good life. My own denomination, like so many once-urban-church movements, slowly targeted suburban and rural rather than city contexts as they multiplied churches in North America and across the globe.

The trends toward city-living and church planting have shifted in recent years. As many cities enter a phase of renewal and economic growth, urban populations are rapidly increasing and perceptions are changing. However, my most formative years of life and ministry were immersed in a time that considered urban life as undesirable at best and fatal at worst. Author Sean Benesh states:

---

[8] Amy L. Sherman, *Kingdom Calling : Vocational Stewardship for the Common Good* (Downers Grove, IL: IVP Books, 2011). 44.

As cities in North America continue to revitalize in
their city centers and central business districts, more
people are moving back into these parts of the city.
This is in contrast to the 1950's through the 1990's
when many of these same districts and
neighborhoods experienced a hollowing out effect as
cities expanded on their edges. Many people moved
to these fringe neighborhoods . . . in hopes of
escaping urban poverty and rising crime. In the
imaginations and reality of many, the term and
descriptor "urban" was synonymous with degraded,
dark, sinful, and dangerous . . . Many cities, like inner
city Portland [OR] can now be described as hipster,
creative, safe, economically and culturally vibrant,
and a great place to live.[9]

As urban descriptors are gaining positive traction, there remains a
need for those who have been schooled in urban fear and subsequently
grown comfortable with the status quo, to embrace the city. With one eye in
the *now* and the other on providing foretastes of the *not yet,* Christ-
followers are poised to transform every aspect of a city—its wealth and
poverty, security and danger, creativity and sin—so often existing side by
side.

A 2011 summer visit to Papua New Guinea brought these co-existing
realities to my attention. I joined a speaking team of Americans and
Australians for the 36th anniversary celebration and conference of PNG's
United Foursquare Women. The conference took place in the highlands, but
on the return trip to our departure city, we spent a day visiting with local
missionaries in the capital city of Port Moresby. Our hosts took us to a
"lookout" just above the harbor known by the same name. Just behind us, a

---

[9] Sean Benesh, *The Urbanity of the Bible* (Portland, OR: Urban Loft Publishers, 2015). 47.

complex of large homes, mansions by the cultural standard, loomed above the city in regal splendor. Occupied primarily by government ministers, their view was incredible with one exception: in the harbor stood "stilt houses," wooden shanties home to the city's poverty-stricken and destitute. Their occupants live above water that serves as a source of food but also as the sewer for garbage and human waste. I stood between the splendor and the squalor wondering how people with the power to make a change—a real change—for those in such plain view, could ignore the obvious. With great disgust and a judgmental tone, I muttered under my breath, "How do *they* (those wealthy creeps!) live with themselves!" As quickly as the words were spoken, God clearly repeated my question, "How do *you* live with yourself?"

The question has reverberated often from my "house on the hill." Situated just east of the city of Portland, Oregon, I have a stunning view of one of the cities wealthiest neighborhoods. However, I do not have to look far to find the city's version of "stilt houses" where many, especially immigrant populations, live in impoverished, below standard conditions; where homeless encampments suffer similar sanitation issues to that of the Port Moresby harbor; and where shelters can't keep up with the long lines of individuals and families looking for a safe place to land for the night. A suburban transplant, I had seldom ventured into such neighborhoods—city blocks of "death and chaos" in the midst of an up and coming hipster, creative, economic and cultural haven like Portland. I, if anyone, needed to be raised from the dead—in mind and conscience. God, indeed, had a plan to inveigle—persuasively free—me from fear and status-quo complacency!

2

Resisting an Edited Gospel: Kingdom and the City

... the goal of God's rescue operation, the main aim of Jesus coming and dying in the first place, is the restoration and transformation of all creation. The slimmed-down version of the gospel is regularly placed within a story in which heaven is the goal—heaven, that is, imagined as a place completely different from the present world, and indeed leaving this present world out of consideration altogether.

~N.T. Wright

Simply Good News: Why the Gospel is News and What Makes it Good

Now after this the Lord appointed seventy others, and sent them in pairs ahead of Him to every city and place where He Himself was going to come.

Luke 10:1

New American Standard Bible

The Spirit of the Lord is on me, because he has anointed me to preach good news to the poor. He has sent me to proclaim freedom for the prisoners and recovery of sight for the blind, to release the oppressed, to proclaim the year of the Lord's favor.

Luke 4:18, 19

Fear and complacency are determining factors of status quo living, but also of "gospel-editing." While culture, education, church history, family history and a myriad of other external and internal forces shape worldview, the result is seen in how the gospel of the kingdom is understood and practiced. My experience in Papua New Guinea stirred awareness and fresh compassion, but God's deep, ample gospel message had begun to emerge a decade prior as my husband and I assumed an urban pastorate in the Northwest. Portland, a progressive and beautiful city of rivers—a city of bridges—served as our initial *bridge* to urban life and ministry.

The "aha moment" of urban life did not take long: I was not in "Kansas" anymore! Never had the steps of my church served as a makeshift Starbucks for a homeless man, kindly offering to hold the door as he greeted the women coming for Bible study. Never had a meth addict barged his way into the building wielding a zucchini (Yes, I said "zucchini!") in sword-like fashion to threaten the pastor as he faithfully delivered God's Word. Never had an elderly cross-dresser attended the senior's Sunday school class.

These were representative of the eclectic neighborhood in which our church was located. The Buckman community also included professionals, artists, business owners, street kids, the poorest of the poor, and the very rich. Often our conservative, traditional church was forced to come to grips with the changing, multi-faceted complexion of our city. We had to learn to become mediators, agents of the gospel—Christ-followers that had a visceral, compassionate response to the present need. Our instincts didn't always lean in the direction of love and acceptance, but God's persistence and patience continued, as one by one—one incredibly uncomfortable visitation at a time—we understood God was revealing himself and the gospel of his kingdom.

Our homeless doorman became a friend of the congregation, a part-time janitor for the church, and tenant of a church-owned apartment only to return, by choice, to the streets. Zucchini Man, as we lovingly dubbed our visiting meth addict, really just wanted a shower and a place to sleep—both of which were provided at a local shelter. Our senior cross-dresser faced a major health crisis and friends from the Sunday school class were there for him, giving him hope for wholeness without stigma or pretense. These and others who followed became a bridge to the city of bridges, helping me cross over to a realization that complex urban issues require a fully orbed gospel of the kingdom.

Awakened to the "Whole" Gospel

Reality . . . it's the quintessential "slap in the face." Like being awakened from a deep sleep when you would rather stay restfully unaware in a cozy bed with a big, soft comforter warming your sweet dreams. That is the reaction I had to the challenge that *my* gospel was anything less than THE GOSPEL of THE KINGDOM! *For goodness sake, Jesus is all anyone needs! Right? Everyone will be just fine if they simply follow Him. Get them to confess their faith and say THE prayer. Now they are going to heaven. Job done. I can crawl back under my comforter.*

This kind of thinking comes at a huge price and runs contrary to the good news of the kingdom. In *Simply Good News,* N.T. Wright describes good news as that which is unexpected in a larger well-known narrative; that which announces everything will now be different; and that a new intermediary waiting period is now filled with hope.[10] Not only is the interim period in which Christ-followers wait for the return of their king filled with hope, it is filled with purpose. The slimmed down or edited version of the gospel relegates hope as far off rather than pursuant of God's mission—a full and rich narrative of his kingdom "on earth as it is in heaven" (Mt 6:1).

The very words, "On earth as it is in heaven," spark a questionable reality. The world is full of horrors. As I was completing this chapter, a

---

[10] N.T. Wright, *Simply Good News: Why the Gospel is News and What Makes it Good* (N. T. Wright, *Simply Good News : Why the Gospel Is News and What Makes It Good*, FIRST EDITION. ed. (New York: HarperCollins Publishers, Inc. 2015), 4.

straight 'A' high school student went on a locker room rampage stabbing five of his classmates;[11] a missing woman was found chained in a storage container on the property of a realtor who, after his arrest, confessed to at least seven murders, including that of the kidnapped woman's boyfriend;[12] and the former economic hub of Syria, Aleppo, was under siege once more as gruesome photos of injured and terrified children surfaced, yet again, in the news.[13] How can heaven remotely have anything to do with earth?

In reality the gospel of the kingdom has everything to do with redemption, healing, and restoration *now* as well as at the Consummation when the fullness of Christ's reign is revealed in a new heaven and a new earth. The present evil has been confronted with God's kingdom through the incarnation of His Son. As N.T. Wright states, "Everything has changed!" At times, the earth is so violent, so repulsively inhumane, it's tempting to believe heaven is altogether *other* than earth. Yet in the face of such extraordinary evil, the church of Jesus Christ is challenged to grasp the all-encompassing gospel, the good news that transforms the "now" to ready humanity for the perfection of that which is "not yet." To believe anything less, cuts away at the unabridged message Jesus proclaimed, edits God's mission on earth, and denies individuals and nations the peace and justice God intended.

The Gospel as Raw Footage

My niece, a film studies major, once reminded me that hard-core movie buffs love to view the uncut version of a movie. "Cuts" make a film more tolerable for the larger audience by limiting the time and content. The editing process removes scenes deemed unnecessary and often alters aspects

---

[11] The Chicago Tribune, "Teen in Utah School Sabbings of Five Classmates Booked on Attempted Murder," http://www.chicagotribune.com/news/nationworld/ct-utah-high-school-stabbing-201story.html, 2016, accessed November 14, 2016.

[12] The New York Times, "South Carolina Cold Case Killer," http://www.nytimes.com/aponline/2016/11/11/us/ap-us-south-carolina-cold-case-killer.html?_r=0, 2016, accessed November 14, 2016.

[13] BBC News, "Syria Conflict: Aleppo Bombarded as Un Warns of Bleak Moment," http://www.bbc.com/news/world-middle-east-38023368, 2016, accessed November 18, 2016.

of the movie to accomplish the most desirable rating. For those working in the industry, seeing the original film is the only way to understand the nuances, significance, and the intent of the screenwriter.

The full-length, unedited version of the "gospel movie" isn't something most Christ-followers know they are missing. Like the majority, I assumed that the just-the-right-length, sellable church version was *THE* story. Comfortably and snugly (maybe even "smugly") I watched a most compelling flick from under my evangelical blanket, never guessing that critical "scenes" (considered unnecessary by some) had been omitted for my viewing pleasure!

Jesus, in training those who proved to be a rather thickheaded bunch, knew how easily his followers would fall into the comfort of a great story. The disciples wanted an edited "we win" plot. Jesus knew they needed to see the whole picture—to understand the Gospel of the Kingdom and the mission to which they were called. Chapter ten of Luke's gospel account provides a glimpse at a major shift of method and place for the purposes of discipleship and mission. Earlier (Lk 9:1), Luke tells how Jesus sent out the twelve, barehanded but with the power and authority to deliver and heal. Shortly after, the Master plainly predicts his death (Lk 9:21-27) and even more clearly addresses the cost of discipleship before appointing seventy-two others to go out into the "harvest field" (Lk 9:57-10:1).

While the directives given in both "sendings" are similar—*don't take anything for the journey, impart peace, proclaim the Kingdom, heal the sick*—one can't help but note the second group is larger (seventy-two rather than twelve) and more organized (go two by two rather than as a group). However, a significant difference not as evident in the text is that, unlike the twelve, Jesus sent the seventy-two beyond Galilee to the other side of the Jordon River. Theologian G. Campbell Morgan explains the dynamic of the regions in which Jesus ministered: Judea was the land of privilege, Samaria the hated place of hostility, Galilee the region of greatest contempt . . . and finally, Perea, or the *other* side of the Jordan, the desolate, neglected area.[14] Campbell notes, "Wherever there is dereliction and desolation on earth, Christ says *that* is where our harvest is."[15]

It is fair to say Jesus saw the harvest against all odds. In the cities and towns of the regions where he ministered, there were "scenes" that caused the disciples to believe these were places too hard for the Gospel to penetrate. They didn't see the harvest Jesus was looking square in the face. Yet, of Samaria, Jesus instructs disciples laden with prejudice, " . . . [Open] your eyes and look at the fields! They are ripe for harvest" (Jn 4:35). Of Galilean towns and villages, home to the scorned "trailer trash" of the day, Jesus says with great compassion, "The harvest is plentiful but the workers are few. Ask the Lord of the harvest, therefore, to send out workers into his harvest field (Mt 9:37)." Of Perea, the neglected "other side of the proverbial tracks" where the marginalized bred indifference from the Jews, the Lord repeats the sentiment: "The harvest is plentiful, but the workers are few. Ask the Lord of the harvest, therefore, to send out workers into his harvest field." Then Jesus adds, "Go! I am sending you out like lambs among wolves (Lk 10:2-3)."

The natural inclination of lambs *and people* is to avoid wolves. If that means neglecting the harvest . . . well . . .! These are symptoms of a misunderstood Gospel of the Kingdom. While the lessons from this story are almost innumerable, I am choosing to focus on Christ's intentional reach to the places that seem the hardest. It is here that Jesus sends his disciples, with their limited view of the uncut gospel, to bring peace, heal the sick, and tell the marginalized, "The kingdom of God has come near you (Lk 10:9)!"

And did they do it? YES! In fact, the "sending" was more successful than they could have imagined. The nearness of the kingdom was manifest in word and deed. The seventy-two would-be preachers reported on their return, "Lord, even the demons submit to us in your name." To this Jesus,

---

[14] *Studies in the Four Gospels, The Gospel According to Luke, 1931 Flemming Revell Publishers, pg 134-137*
[15] ibid. 136.

replied, "I saw Satan fall like lightning from heaven. I have given you authority to trample on snakes and scorpions and to overcome all the power of the enemy; nothing will harm you (Lk 10:18-19)."

Author Jack Levison, in a devotional on the Holy Spirit, reminds his readers of Jesus' prayer admonition to "Ask, and it will be given you; search and you will find; knock and the door will be opened for you . . . Is there anyone among you who, if your child asks for a fish, will give a snake instead of a fish? Or if the child asks for an egg, will give a scorpion? If you then, who are evil, know how to give good gifts to your children, how much more will the heavenly Father give the Holy Spirit to those who ask Him (Lk 11:9-13 NRSV)!" Levinson contends that here and in Luke chapter ten, "snakes and scorpions aren't just bad presents. They are symbols of demonic power, of Satanic authority, of bared-teeth evil."[16] Authority over such evil was given by Christ, maintained through prayer, and acted on through the power of the Holy Spirit. This is the unedited version of a whole gospel—going where Christ sends to bring wholeness, healing, and transformation to the immediate and eternal needs of those he sees and loves.

Face to Face with "Scorpions and Snakes"

In the spring of 2010, I visited an organized homeless encampment with a group of graduate students. Under the shadow of Fresno, California's twisted freeway overpasses, the students attentively listened to the encampment's director innumerate the multi-faceted demands and rewards of serving the homeless. As if on cue, a half-dressed woman soliciting across the street caught everyone's attention. Her scantily clad body was less of a distraction than the illicit, seductive movements used to proposition each of the men standing on her "corner." In what seemed like the blink of an eye, she was suddenly on our side of the street, her presence unavoidable among a small band of students who were there to learn *about* the plight of homelessness, not interact *with* one of its victims. "Shadow," a sadly

---

[16] John R. Levison, *40 Days with the Holy Spirit : Fresh Air for Every Day* (Brewster, MA: Paraclete Press, 2015).

appropriate name, slithered around the circle asking for change and chanting repetitive phrases in which the only recognizable word was "Jesus."

The name of Jesus represents love, power, healing, and comfort. But the name Shadow spoke embodied something quite the opposite, regardless of the like pronunciation. Clearly high on drugs, possibly demon-possessed, mentally ill—or both—the woman nudged her way inside our small "educational huddle." The students, at the moment grateful for that designated status, waited for Dr. White, our fearless professor, to take the lead. He told Shadow we could not give her money, but we would very much like to pray for her. She reluctantly granted permission and with an otherworldly voice shrieked, "Don't touch me! Don't touch me!" This woman, who made her drug money by the touch of sordid men, was terrified by compassionate hands that represented, in a very real way, Christ's hand of love and deliverance.

Shadow needed his touch. She needed a gospel powerful enough to transform heart *and* circumstance; a gospel effective enough to push back the darkness that had placed her so far from the Light her very name gave evidence to her bondage. Jesus came preaching this gospel. Author, Mark Gornik notes:

> In his inaugural and programmatic sermon . . . Jesus announces the gospel bound up with his person, as the new beginning for the poor, the oppressed, and the city. Citing passages from Isaiah 53 and 61, Jesus proclaims,
>
> > The Spirit of the Lord is on me,
> > because he has anointed me
> > to preach good news to the poor.
> > He has sent me to proclaim freedom for the prisoners
> > and recovery of sight for the blind,
> > to release the oppressed,

to proclaim the year of the Lord's favor. (Luke 4:18, 19)[17]
Immediately, Jesus follows with a bold statement: "Today this scripture is fulfilled in your hearing (Lk 4:21)."

Clearly, Jesus *was* the new beginning not only in a spiritual sense, but also in the sense that he fully intended to "alter the physical conditions of the people of Israel."[18] His words brought "a holistic dimension into the mission that Jesus [set] out for himself."[19] In a language and imagery of the Old Testament Year of Jubilee, "the gospel makes all things right—the poor are lifted up, the prisoners are released, sins are forgiven, and the curse of sin is reversed . . . Christ's proclamation of the gospel [is] both personally and socially transforming."[20]

For all the "Shadows" and "Zucchini Men," there is a message of good news—healing for body, soul, mind, and spirit—waiting to be proclaimed *now*. For every town and village, whether privileged, hated, held in contempt, or marginalized there is a message of hope--Good News has the power to change . . . if we are willing to resist an edited gospel of our own making.

The kingdom is now. The gospel is BIG. The city is waiting. We have been sent.

---

[17] Mark R. Gornik, *To Live in Peace: Biblical Faith and the Changing Inner City* (Grand Rapids, MI: W.B. Eerdmans Pub., 2002), 27-28.

[18] Robert Kysar, *Called to Care: Biblical Images for Social Ministry* (Minneapolis: Fortress Press, 1991), 33.

[19] Christopher J. H. Wright, *The Mission of God : Unlocking the Bible's Grand Narrative* (Downers Grove, Ill.: IVP Academic, 2006).

[20] Gornik, 28.

3

Resisting Injustice: Mission and Shalom

For a child has been born—for us!
The gift of a son—for us!
He'll take over the running of the world.
His names will be: Amazing Counselor, Strong God, Eternal Father,
Prince of Wholeness [Peace].
His ruling authority will grow, and there'll be no limits to the wholeness he
brings.
He'll rule from the historic David throne over that promised Kingdom.
He'll put that kingdom on a firm footing and keep it going with
fair dealing and right living, beginning now and lasting always.

Isaiah 9:6, 7
The Message Bible

It isn't unusual to find my husband and me hanging out in the foyer
after church. Old habits die hard. After 25 years of pastoral ministry, we
learned that the space between the "sanctuary" and the exit doors is where
human interaction actually has a chance to move beyond a mere greeting.
One such after-service encounter led us, now as church members, to a
couple standing alone near the information "wall" (some churches have
counters—we have a wall!). As we engaged in conversation, we discovered

they were newly retired and had been attending church in a community south of Portland. The drive to the suburbs from the urban center had become a little too much, and they made the decision to find something closer to home. Out of curiosity, we asked how it was they chose to visit *this* church. (Asking nosey questions—another hard-to-break habit for pastor types!)

The interaction had been pretty typical up to a point. We discovered a few family factoids, the occupation they had retired from, how long they'd been members at their previous place of worship, where they lived, etc. Then, they dove headfirst into a unique story regarding church choice. Apparently, their pastor of many years was walking through the neighborhood a few weeks prior to their first visit. He stopped in front of our building musing over this odd-shaped facility with no obvious name but a clearly displayed slogan, *The Art of Living Sideways*. As he stood on the sidewalk with a dazed question mark on his face, a local house-less neighbor piped up, "Man, it's a church! You should go there. The people are really kind and they *like* truly care about this community!"

The *Alongsiders Community,* one of several urban congregations in Portland, has found that embodying Christ to a neighborhood requires incarnation and imagination. The removal of an exterior wall and addition of several glass garage doors open the building to a large public patio, coffee bar, and open-air room for viewing local sporting events with neighbors. Alongside the building is a food pantry configured much like a grocery store that operates on three Sunday afternoons every month. The rest of the building is the remains of an older church facility, that to tell the truth, looks like a big box. It is no wonder the walk-by pastor was perplexed! The confusion ended quickly with the witness of our street-friend who had encountered a church living life sideways, coming alongside neighbors . . . bringing wholeness—signage optional!

God's mission for the church can be described no better than in the Hebrew word *shalom*. Derived from the root word for *wholeness*,[21] shalom characterizes much more than an absence of strife. It is the biblical expression for peace, justice, abundance, and security. "It means a combination of righteousness and justice, making things the way they should be *in* people, *between* people, and *for* people"[22]—a return to pre-Fall Eden. One theologian notes that shalom is "the webbing together of God, humans, and all creation in justice, fulfillment and delight . . . [a] universal flourishing, wholeness, and delight.[23] In contrast to the chaos that existed before God created Eden, and once again after sin entered the world, shalom is a picture of what life should be when Jesus is in the picture.

Jesus completely changed the picture. His initial proclamation, in Luke chapter four, announced that "the year of the Lord's favor" had just made its debut . . . because he had made his. (If his audience had not been so dumbfounded, there may have been shouts of "Jubilee!") This was incredible news—the commencement of Jesus' mission on earth.[24] Author Mark Gornick explains the importance of Christ's words in relationship to Isaiah's prophecy:

> The "good news" is the Jubilee message of [Lk] 4:18-19, a
> citation of Isaiah 61:1-2. In this text, Isaiah links God's new
> day for the poor with the promise of urban recovery: "They
> will rebuild the ancient ruins and restore the places long
> devastated; they will renew the ruined cities that have been

---

[21] Wilhelm Gesenius, James Strong, and Samuel Prideaux Tregelles, *Gesenius' Hebrew and Chaldee Lexicon to the Old Testament Scriptures : Numerically Coded to Strong's Exhaustive Concordance, with an English Index of More Than 12,000 Entries* (Grand Rapids: Baker Book House, 1979). 825.

[22] Randy White, *Encounter God in the City : Onramps to Personal and Community Transformation* (Downers Grove, Ill.: IVP Books, 2006). http://www.loc.gov/catdir/toc/ecip0612/2006013027.html. 53.

[23] Cornelius Plantinga, Jr., "Educating for Shalom: Our Calling as a Christian College," in Nicholas Wolterstorff, Clarence W. Joldersma, and Gloria Goris Stronks, *Educating for Shalom: Essays on Christian Higher Education* (Grand Rapids, MI: W.B. Eerdmans Pub. Co., 2004), quoted in Sherman, 34.

[24] Robert Kysar, *Called to Care : Biblical Images for Social Ministry* (Minneapolis: Fortress Press, 1991). 33.

> devastated for generations." (Is 61:4) . . . the [good news]
> empowers the poor, the outcast, and the forgotten to share
> in God's redemption of the city.[25]

For those who had lost any hope of restoration and redemption, Jesus became the "good news" . . . the representation of God's favor . . . the gospel of peace (Is 52:7, Rom 10:15). Scripture declares, "The Word became flesh and blood, and moved into the neighborhood . . . This one-of-a-kind God-Expression, who exists at the very heart of the Father, has made him plain as day (Jn 1:14-18 MSG)."

If there was any doubt regarding God's heart to restore shalom to his people, Jesus' proximity and grace-filled works were live demonstrations. He infiltrated cities, villages, and communities with healing and forgiveness. He brought wholeness (peace) to the outcast and the shamed, to the poor and the rich, allowing people to flourish in the midst of a deteriorating society. He made possible the delight of intimate relationship with God, love for neighbor and self, and care for all of his creation. Resonate with the meaning of shalom, the Greek word for peace, *eirene*, is descriptive of harmony, safety, and security, but most simply put, it means "to set at one again."[26] It is the reconciling factor for all relationships made possible because Jesus moved into the neighborhood.

Shalom Defined by Justice

Peace that "sets at one again" is good news for every neighborhood and every city. Shalom is God's unbridled love come near, unrestrained grace that resists the injustice of our fractured cities. It is what most of us would love to see happen, but have forgotten that God's mission, and therefore our mission, includes a calling to justice.

---

[25] Mark R. Gornik, *To Live in Peace : Biblical Faith and the Changing Inner City* (Grand Rapids, Mich.: W.B. Eerdmans Pub., 2002). 28.

[26] Carl Ludwig Wilibald Grimm et al., *A Greek-English Lexicon of the New Testament : Being Grimm's Wilke's Clavis Novi Testamenti* (Grand Rapids: Baker Book House, 1977). 182.

Isaiah chapter nine, a prophetic promise to Israel of a coming Messiah, describes the Savior as a Prince of Wholeness and states emphatically that there will be no end to the wholeness he brings. "Fair dealing and right living"—righteousness or justice—are hallmarks of his boundless peace. Shalom, putting all the pieces back into one, expressly manifests justice—or that which "[sets] things right."[27] Oneness, or wholeness and rightness (righteousness), form a biblical perspective that surpasses "beauty pageant world peace" and gives way to the natural partnership of ideology with practice.

The authors of *The Justice Calling* so aptly communicate the *idea* of justice, and our *response* to justice, in Jesus' reply to a religion scholar's question of which command in God's law is most important:

> The two greatest commandments identified by Jesus—to love God and to love your neighbor as yourself [Mt 22:35-40]—are the flip side of the two most prevalent sins throughout Scripture: idolatry and injustice. Failing to love God leads to idolatry, while failing to love others leads to injustice. Another way of putting this is to say that the call to love God and love our neighbors is a call to righteousness and justice.[28]

If, then, we are a people who actively love God, we will also actively love our neighbor by seeking justice *for* our neighbor.

Tim Keller, pastor and theologian, further explains the significance of justice by combining the two most prominent Hebrew words for justice. *Mishpat* describes a just God, a just man, and a just system that maintains equitable punishment and care for every member of society. This word is used often in reference to those most vulnerable—the poor, widows, orphans, and immigrants. God is willfully determined that these receive

---

[27] Bethany H. Hoang, *The Justice Calling : Where Passion Meets Perseverance.* 11.
[28] Ibid. 17.

what is due them *and* equally concerned that those who choose to ignore or exploit them receive their just due.

The other Hebrew word is *tzadeqah.* Usually translated as "righteousness," this type of justice portrays a life of right relationship with God that issues into righteous living—that which is "profoundly social."[29] It encompasses our personal touch, individually or collectively, on our neighbor—the person next door or the homeless man across town. The sharing of our resources, talents, and time with those less fortunate are marks of a *just* life.

Keller reminds us, "Justice includes not only the righting of wrongs but generosity and social concern, especially toward the poor and vulnerable."[30] Therefore, *mishpat* and *tsadeqah* combined are best expressed in English as "social justice."[31] Should the church choose to deprive itself of either the vocal or action-oriented proclamation of faith, we will fall short of the mission God has in mind.

Complete Justice, Unlikely Peace

Perhaps the greatest resistance to the pursuit of justice as integral to shalom is not the concept itself, but rather what we imagine it may entail. Simply hearing the words "social justice" in relationship to Christian discipleship, stirred up in my mind's eye images of crowds with angry faces, carrying signs of protest. Indeed, at times, the church has engaged such activities—I have. Recently, in my city, many pastors and church members participated in a march after the senseless shooting of a young black man. There is a time and a place and validity to such action.

However, to balance what we usually think of as a "fight for justice," Scripture provides a glimpse of justice that is at the core of God's heart. I must warn you that it comes with a huge personal requirement. Much like

---

[29] Tim Keller, "What Is Biblical Justice,"
http://www.relevantmagazine.com/god/practical-faith/what-biblical-justice, 2012, accessed February 12, 2013.
[30] Ibid.
[31] Ibid.

the religious scholar who asked Jesus what the most important commandment was, true justice costs us our religious piety. Listen to these verses from the prophet Isaiah:

> Quit your worship charades. I can't stand your trivial religious games: monthly conferences, weekly Sabbaths, and special meetings—I can't stand one more! Meetings for this, meetings for that. I hate them! You've worn me out! I'm sick of your religion, religion, religion, while you go right on sinning. When you put on your next prayer performance, I'll be looking the other way. No matter how long or loud or often you pray, I'll not be listening. And do you know why? Because you are tearing people to pieces, and your hands are bloody. Go home and wash up. Clean up your act. Sweep your lives clean of your evildoings so I don't have to look at them any longer. Say no to wrong. Learn to do good. Work for justice. Help the down-and-out. Stand up for the homeless. Go to bat for the defenseless. (Is 1:13-17 The Message)

The same Old Testament author goes on to pen audacious descriptions of shalom and justice in the coming Leader of Israel. In chapter eleven, God declares Israel's king with "a mere breath from his lips will topple the wicked. Each morning he'll pull on sturdy work clothes and boots, and build righteousness and faithfulness in the land (Is 11:4-5 The Message)." Then, when just decisions are made regarding the needy and the poor—when shalom is established—"The wolf will live with the lamb, the leopard will lie down with the goat . . . the infant will play near the cobra's den . . . they will neither harm nor destroy . . . (Is 11:6-9)."

Rather than a fight for justice, "complete justice, in brief, ushers in unlikely peace."[32] Nothing is more unlikely than a predator and livestock or humans living, lying, and playing together. What a picture of the Father's

---

[32] Levison. 86.

intended shalom! Resistance to such unmitigated oneness and rightness is determined, in part, by my willingness to come face to face with my own trivial religious games—my Christian performance that seems *right,* but leaves a lot of "bloody body parts" in its self-righteous, judgmental wake! It sounds harsh and almost as if God is being a bit too hard on his people. After all, they were at least faithful to go to "church" meetings; they were "observant" of special days; and they gave offerings.

What appeared to be extreme devotion was anything but. Their hearts were empty and their hands full . . . of blood. The people did their religious duty and then eagerly participated in murder, rape, and oppression with no punishment. The "religious" leaders were complicit, and God insists they go home, wash up (repent), stop doing evil, and *learn* to do right—seek justice and defend the oppressed. *Learn* to do justice.

I would like to believe that in the conversion experience, the Holy Spirit creates a justice-meter and a justice-reflex. Instead, I (and maybe you too) have found myself increasingly calloused to the needy. I've noticed that religious meetings have sometimes taken the place of "practicing" true religion that, according to Scripture, is to "look after the orphans and widows in their distress and to keep oneself from being polluted by the world (Jas 1:27)." The pollution of a godless, uncaring society is oh so effortlessly mirrored in believers with a propensity to resist justice or ignore it entirely.

Shalom: Justice in Action

One of the joys of my life is the facilitation of a network of leaders who are foster care advocates. Some of the network members are foster parents, others advocate as mediators between state institutions and faith-based non-profits. During a recent call, the members, three of whom were facing a current foster-related crisis, noted the ups and downs of the system, the trauma induced suffering of kids, and the challenges of adopting a foster child. In their efforts to bring awareness and resource to parents, leaders, and churches, they were the ones needing encouragement.

The "at-the-moment" personal support they needed began with a single comment, "You have to be ALL-IN! There's no halfway commitment in this ministry." A resounding "Amen" was uttered from the lips of every member. The conversation that followed brought incredible affirmation and resolve: their obedience matters. This group of radical saints knows that even if time with a child is cut short, obeying God—being present to "look after the orphans"—makes an unforgettable difference in the life of one child.

The prophet Micah asserts that justice is an action word. "He has shown you, O man, what is good. And what does the Lord require of you? To act justly and to love mercy and to walk humbly with your God (Mi 6:8)." A condensed version of biblical precepts, this verse *shows* God's requirement for man as matter-of-fact in light of what he has already revealed. Yet, justice cannot be reduced to personal piety or moral excellence. Bruce Watke, an Old Testament scholar, offers this helpful definition of "all in" justice, "The righteous (*saddiq*) are willing to disadvantage themselves to advantage the community; the wicked are willing to disadvantage the community to advantage themselves."[33] Our cities and communities are full of people who take advantage of the amenities: parks, shopping, business services, senior services, educational institutions, arts and music, housing, street maintenance, garbage pick-up, police and fire protection, etc. Of course, these offerings are supposed to be used and enjoyed—even expected—but there is a dimension of shalom that will never be realized until we are personally willing to sacrifice our time and convenience—maybe even a few meetings—to make sure that the community is advantaged by the "Prince of Peace." At least in part, this requires followers of Christ to value and work toward equity for all their neighbors. To pursue justice in such a

---

[33] Bruce K. Waltke, *The Book of Proverbs*, 2 vols., *The New International Commentary on the Old Testament* (Grand Rapids, Mich.: William B. Eerdmans Pub., 2004). Quoted in Timothy J. Keller, *Center Church: Doing Balanced, Gospel-Centered Ministry in Your City* (Grand Rapids, MI: Zondervan, 2012), 321.

way that all things are "set right" and all things (and people) are "set at one again."

Author Howard Snyder explains shalom and justice as it is fulfilled in Christ. He states:

> Israel's prophets promised that God would in time send a special servant-king, the Messiah, who would actually accomplish God's redemptive plan. Through the Messiah, God would himself bring perfect *shalom,* as pictured so beautifully in Isaiah 11 and many other passages. The first covenant would be superseded by a New Covenant through which sin would be atoned for, God's Spirit poured out, God's law written on human hearts, and God's purposes finally fulfilled. God's kingdom of justice and *shalom* would come in fullness. This was prefigured already in Abraham's encounter with Melchizedek ("King of righteousness" [justice]), who was "king of Salem" (a form of *shalom*) (Gen 14-18-20).[34]

God's mission of peace—oneness, wholeness, flourishing, delight, abundance, security and yes, justice—was his intention from the beginning, fulfilled in Christ and to-be-completed at his return. Until then, it is vital for his church to be agents of shalom. The external injustice we face daily— inequity in education, poverty, homelessness, human trafficking, crime, corrupt government, etc.—cannot change until our hearts grasp the call to live in the light of true religion that takes action on behalf of those less privileged.

Shalom, the complete and overwhelming peace that justly puts life together again, can seem an ethereal almost wraith concept in a broken world where the most vulnerable continue to be victimized and ignored. The elements of impossibility and the human condition were indeed the purpose

---

[34] Howard A. Snyder, *Small Voice, Big City: The Challenge of Urban Mission* (Skyforest, CA: Urban Loft Publishers, 2016). 243

for the opening story of this chapter. While the identity of the homeless man with kind words about the church that doesn't look like a church is unknown, many like him have experienced hunger *set right* and relationships *set at one* again. "Living sideways, coming alongside neighbors" is a privilege. Caring for those who face food insecurity goes beyond sacks of groceries. It is a means of restoring dignity, offering friendship, and, in degrees less than most would consider significant, a community of belonging and safety. The guests who frequent the Food Pantry are welcomed into a Starbucks-like space. Small round tables dot the large meeting room turned grocery store, and "free" pastries line serving trays ready to be devoured over conversation with each other and with the pantry volunteers. The conversations reveal stories. The stories reveal people made in the image of God.

These image-bearers, like you and me, long for the wholeness only Christ can ultimately provide. Remarkably, he communicates and exercises his distinct definition of *shalom* through his disciples. Snyder reminds us, "As God's counterculture, the church is not merely to be in the world; it is to pursue the mission of God in the world. It is the agent of God's kingdom in bringing all things under the headship of Jesus Christ (Eph 1:10)."[35] The mission of shalom is nothing less than audacious. One day, the wolf will live with the lamb in peace. Until that day, God has invited us to practice true religion—not just have meetings; love our neighbors—not just live in proximity; and resist injustice with shalom in the boldness of those called by Christ himself.

---

[35] Ibid,

4

Resisting Systemic Sin: History and the Spiritual Battle

Cities are the defining artifacts of civilization. All the achievements and failings of humanity are here. Civic buildings, monuments, archives and institutions are the touchstones by which our cultural heritage is passed from one generation to the next. We shape the city, then it shapes us. Today, almost half the global population lives in cities. By 2030, the proportion is likely to be two-thirds.

~ John Reader

Cities

Practicing the lessons of history is a description of God's tender arms—one around the church, the other around the community. History helps us "get" the church so we can "get into" the community.

~ Ray Bakke

Global Christian History Lecture

God sacrificed Jesus on the altar of the world to clear that world of sin . . . God decided on this course of action in full view of the public . . . This is not only clear, but it's now—this is current history!

The Czech Republic is known for its castles and cathedrals. Standing as if history itself has come to life in the present, these ancient structures offer their lessons of grandeur and decay . . . and, in many cases, testify to the power of modern renovation skills. Magnificent cathedrals, such as St. Vitas, located inside the Prague Castle Complex, literally hold the bones of bishops and kings. Remnants of castles still in the process of restoration, such as Točník, or decidedly restored castles, such as the castle city of Český Krumlov, equally impress. One can see literally, or with minor levels of imagination, the moats, draw bridges, dungeons, and grand banquet rooms filled with the activity of kings and knights—or the torture of its enemies! Resident or tourist, it is difficult to escape the palpable awe in the architecture that lends modern guests a small taste of life in a bygone era.

This state of inspirational wonder is something I've experienced often. Our son and his family have lived in Prague for the past eighteen years. My husband and I can't seem to stay away from the "land of our grandchildren," making the trip over a dozen times. Not coincidentally, it is also the land of my husband's family heritage; he is the grandchild of Czech immigrants. Family ties, current and historic, keep us connected with this magical Eastern European country and allow us the privilege of investigating centuries old structures that played significant roles in the built and cultural environment of ancient cities.

In contrast to the magnificent castles and cathedrals we've visited over the years, Bethlehem Chapel in Prague is a less imposing structure, but one of great import. The chapel, almost entirely a reproduction of a spacious but modest building, was home to the preaching of Jan Hus (John Huss) an early reformer of the church. Huss, who also served as the dean of the Faculty of Philosophy at the University of Prague, was exposed to and influenced by the writings of English reformer, John Wycliffe, through the university's close ties with their counterparts at Oxford. Both Wycliffe and

Huss were disturbed by the growing corruption of the clergy, "whom [Huss] called 'the Lord's fat ones,' and accused of fornication, absenteeism, and enriching themselves at the expense of the people."[36]

These accusations came at the height of the conciliar movement in which the Catholic Church attempted to address a divided papacy, known as the Great Schism, and the practices of simony and nepotism "without substantially challenging accepted Christian dogma."[37] Huss himself sought only to return the church to its former integrity. However, it soon became apparent that practices, such as that of preaching in the vernacular, communion "in both kinds" (bread *and* cup for all believers), the banning of indulgences, and the consideration of Christ as the *only* head of the Church were not acceptable in a system that was still focused on the papacy. Huss was eventually burned at the stake for heresy at the Council of Constance.[38]

This very sketchy account of an incredibly detailed and intricate story of political and church history illustrates what modern urban writers refer to as "systemic sin." Huss, and the reformers who came before and after, tackled head on the exploitation wielded by those charged with the wellbeing of their citizens/parishioners. Observation, not judgment, leads us to believe that the institutions of our day are also susceptible to creating, sometimes unknowingly, systems that harm rather than serve or heal.

Beyond Individual Choice

After prompting the imagination toward castles, cathedrals, and early church reformation, the intention is not to sensationalize evil or convince the reader that he might be thrown in a dungeon or that she might one day be burned at the stake! Nevertheless, church leaders from multiple backgrounds are growing increasingly aware that there is a systemic

---

[36] Justo L. González, *The Story of Christianity. Volume 1, the Early Church to the Reformation*, Rev. and updated [ed.], 2nd ed. (New York: HarperCollins, 2010). 415-417.
[37] Ibid. 407.
[38] Ibid. 417-419.

dimension of sin that goes beyond individual moral choices.[39] For Christ followers, the unfair treatment and inequality suffered by particular groups of people, the vulnerable, and the poor is reason to consciously observe, deliberately discover, and intentionally serve those caught in a "networked web"[40] of injustice.

In the previous chapter, biblical shalom painted a picture of God's best intention for our cities. Marred as they are by both individual and systemic sin, the urban trajectory continues to be characteristic of God's mission.[41] On the opening page of his book *Cities*, anthropology fellow John Reader[42] acknowledges that by the year 2030 the proportion of the global population living in cities is likely to be two-thirds.[43] Readers' prediction, made in 2004, is substantiated by United Nations statistics for 2016, which state that over fifty-four percent of the world's population currently live in urban settlements and by 2030 these cities are projected to house sixty per cent of people globally with one in three people living in cities of at least half a million inhabitants.[44] Bringing people together, creating community, and the restoration and redemption of those places seems to be God's specialty.

Wherever people are, there will be the image of God's goodness and the marks of sin. The convolution comes as people enter the systems of power that have taken on a life of their own. The book of Ephesians reminds us that we are to "be strong in the Lord and in his mighty power. Put on the full armor of God, so that you can take your stand against the devil's schemes. For our struggle is not against flesh and blood, but against the rulers, against the authorities, against the powers of this dark world and

[39] Ronald J. Sider, Philip N. Olson, and Heidi Rolland Unruh, *Churches That Make a Difference : Reaching Your Community with Good News and Good Works* (Grand Rapids, Mich.: Baker Books, 2002). 94.

[40] White. 66.

[41] Benesh. 24.

[42] Library of Congress, "Contributor Biographical Information for Cities," http://catdir.loc.gov/catdir/enhancements/fy0628/2005440738-b.html, 2004, accessed March 10, 2016.

[43] John Reader, *Cities* (New York, NY: Grove Press, 2004). 1.

[44] United Nations, "The World's Cities in 2016," http://www.un.org/en/development/desa/population/publications/pdf/urbanization/the_worlds_cities_in_2016_data_booklet.pdf, 2016, accessed (March 10, 2016).

against spiritual forces of evil in the heavenly realms (Eph 6:10-12)." While not giving way to unrealistic blaming of otherworldly powers of evil for every social ill known to man, we would be foolish to not recognize that we do contend with spiritual forces beyond the human manifestation of sin.

Understanding the ways in which principalities and powers intersect and operate through ordinary human institutions is not always easy. Christians often see the surface of deep issues (the tip of the iceberg) and make seemingly legitimate assessments that may not probe far enough. Author Mark Gornik helps with a brief explanation of *powers:*

> If the purpose of the reign of God is to reconcile all things (2 Cor. 5:19; Eph. 1:10; Col 1:20), then the primary objective of the powers is to oppose all that supports, advances, and constitutes reconciliation. The "rulers of this age" are servitors of injustice, transpersonal expressions of exploitation, and agents of oppression. Mortally wounded by the cross, they still try to mawl [*sic*] people and communities through "exclusion" and "domination" (I Cor. 2:8; Gal. 4:1-3; Rev. 2:12-13). Exclusionary in aim and intention, the "principalities and powers" can be embedded in political, social, and economic institutions of the inner city.[45]

Though structural or systemic sin can be found in every sector, system, and strata of a society, it is not to say that all structures are evil. Of course, good is also found in such places as government agencies, financial corporations, and religious institutions. However, when these intentionally or unintentionally work to exclude or dominate—alone or in tandem—it is the response of believers to look for root causes and challenge their own theological framework.

---

[45] Mark Gornik, *To Live in Peace : Biblical Faith and the Changing Inner City.* (Grand Rapids, MI: Eerdmans Publishing, 2002). 55.

Challenging our Belief System

The church is in no way immune to systemic sin, which sometimes originates in its own well-constructed religious traditions. The Apostle Paul, in his letter to the Galatians, describes a heated face-to-face confrontation with Peter who was "clearly out of line (Gal 2:11 The Message)." Peter, the man who experienced a direct revelation from God regarding the church's acceptance of non-Jews and defended Gentile believers to the "institutional" church council, apparently lapsed in his convictions. A "conservative Jewish clique [that was] pushing the old system of circumcision (Gal 2:12 The Message)" showed up in Antioch and Peter didn't want to ruffle any feathers. While he had done so on many occasions, he refused to eat with the non-Jews in their midst. Peter's poor example led the entire Antioch church, and even Barnabas, into some serious issues with hypocrisy, exclusion—and, yes, racism.

A system, religious or otherwise, that promotes exclusion gives way to a culture that, sometimes too easily, buckles under popular opinion. Peter and Barnabas didn't recognize the old system of circumcision as a "power" slowly eating away at the integrity and mission of God's people. Needless to say, if Paul hadn't jutted his jaw and come nose to nose with Peter proclaiming the truth, "We Jews know that we have no advantage of birth over non-Jewish sinners [and we] know very well that we are not set right with God by rule-keeping but only through personal faith in Jesus Christ (Gal 2:15 The Message)," God's continued work among the people of the world may have been woefully delayed. Hopefully, after being set straight, Peter and Barnabas pulled a few extra chairs up to the table and shared some matzo ball and ham soup with the Gentiles!

For today's church, we *know* that inclusion of all people is at the center of God's heart. Yet, our churches and communities are still largely segregated. In my beautiful city, I was surprised to learn that an exclusion law, enacted when Oregon was a territory and not yet a state, had not been rescinded until 1926,[46] and the right for blacks to vote was not ratified until 1959.[47] These restrictions in the "system" fostered an unwelcome tone toward African Americans in Portland's early history that has played out over the decades.

A long pattern of discrimination against African Americans manifested itself in segregation. Restaurants and theaters adhered to a "Jim Crow"—equal but separate—attitude well into the sixties. "Segregated housing was instituted by local realtors meeting around a conference table. As a matter of 'ethics,' local realtors would refuse to rent or sell homes to blacks outside of specific areas."[48] Currently, Portland's gentrification has pushed many African Americans, along with immigrant and refugee populations, from the city center to what has become known as the "Other Portland"—an area east of Interstate 205 lacking needed services, grocery stores, banks, good schools, and a general sense of safety.[49] Racial tensions are at an all-time high in Portland, as they are at present in our nation. In the United States, those who are old enough, feel as though they are reliving the sixties and seventies—this time in vivid HD color.

Racism is one of the multiple ways in which systemic sin affects society. Issues of fair education, poverty, homelessness, human trafficking, gang violence, addiction, and the multitude of social concerns we face are woven into the fabric of corrupt systems. These are complex problems and the church can find itself immobilized—simply not knowing what to do. "Adam and Eve's sin messed up absolutely everything, implying that *both* individuals and systems are broken."[50] In order for real, transformative

---

[46] L.A. Barrie, "Timeimage, Reflections of Portland: Portland's Black Community and the Church," *The Neighborhood History Project, Bureau of Parks and Recreation* 1, no. 2 (1979). 36.

[47] Dick Pintarich, ed., *The Struggle of Blacks in Oregon, Great and Minor Moments in Oregon's History*, ed. Dick Pintarich (Portland: New Oregon Publishers, Inc., 2008). 288.

[48] Ibid. 293.

[49] Willamette Week Corey Pein, "The Other Portland," http://www.wweek.com/portland/article-18071-the-other-portland.html, 2017, accessed Jan 31, 2017.

[50] Steve Corbett, and Brian Fikkert, *When Helping Hurts : How to Alleviate Poverty without Hurting the Poor-- and Yourself* (Chicago, IL: Moody Publishers, 2009). 84.

change to take place, we will need to learn the "whys" behind the way we think and live. Many times the answers can be seen in historic systemic sin. Author Robert Linthicum comments on the church's state of oblivion to Satan's strategies:

> First, those who provide the primary leadership to the systems are ripe for seduction. They tend to overestimate their own power because they are convinced they are in control. Second, the church is woefully ignorant of this strategy. The city church places its primary effort into individuals and its secondary effort into church and family groupings. The church thus leaves the field open to Satan for exerting spiritual influence on both the city's systems and its interior spirituality.[51]

The culture of a community and its churches are linked together with a history that affects both. Where history leaches the worst, it is up to the church to bring God's best.

Challenging a Political System

Israel was intended to be a prototype of God's people bringing the best in the worst of situations. They were commissioned by God's covenant with Abraham to bless all peoples and nations of the earth (Gn 12:1-3). However, a long history of unfaithfulness finds Israel in a place of captivity and living in the midst of evil systems. Babylon and King Nebuchadnezzer had successfully laid siege and the Israelites were living in a harsh and pagan land, quite bereft of their former freedoms. Theologian Christopher J.H. Wright reminds us:

> On the plane of human history, it was perfectly true that the exiles of Judah were the victims of Nebuchadnezzar's

---

[51] Robert C. Linthicum, *City of God, City of Satan: A Biblical Theology of the Urban Church* (Grand Rapids, MI: Zondervan, 1991), in Harvie M. Conn and Manuel Ortiz, *Urban Ministry: The Kingdom, the City & the People of God* (Downers Grove, IL: InterVarsity Press, 2001. 367.

imperial conquest. From the perspective of God's
sovereignty, however, they were still a people in the hands
of their God. The sword of Nebuchadnezzar was being
wielded by the God of Israel. With this perspective Jeremiah
urged the exiles to settle down and accept the reality of their
circumstances. God had exiled them to Babylon; they had
better treat it as home for the time being (vv. 5-6). They
would not be home in two years (as false prophets were
saying); they would be in Babylon for two generations.
Babylon was not their permanent home, but it was their
present home.[52]

Wright goes on to explain that captivity was far from a "despairing
resignation to their fate. Jeremiah [tells them]: Increase in number there, do
not decrease"[53] (Jer 29:6). God's Abrahamic promise of increase and
blessing would continue even in this strange land.

Pivotal to the fulfillment of this promise was Israel's willingness to
settle into their new surroundings and live the mission to which God had
called them. The prophet further instructs the people to build houses, plant
gardens, and marry (Jer 29:4-6). Then, in what might have seemed an
unfathomable concept, the Prophet admonished the victims of exploitation
to "seek the peace and prosperity of the city to which [God had] carried
[them] into exile. Pray to the Lord for it, because if it prosper[ed], [they] too
[would] prosper (Jer 29:7)."

Far from the day when Jesus would instruct us to pray for our
enemies (Mt 5:43), Jeremiah seems to be crossing the line, religiously and
culturally. Yet, these God-words reminded Israel that his promise was not
just for the future. God's promise for them and for the nations of the world
was happening now—in the very place they found themselves broadsided by
regret, shame, sadness, frustration, and anger. In this place, God would

---

[52] Wright. 99.
[53] Ibid. 99.

bless them and make them a blessing . . . if they would pray. In a position of servitude—a milieu of evil systems—God asked that they participate in the building of a community, that they represent the best in the worst of the city, and pray earnestly for its welfare and prosperity.

It is likely that a God who "worked the system" for the blessing of Israel *and* their "temporary" home city, would do the same for us. God has not left us defenseless against the powers of world systems or spiritual forces of evil. He gave us "system-resistant" armor that centers us in a kingdom theology and makes us conflict preventive.[54] A belt of truth, a breastplate of righteousness, shoes of peace, a shield of faith, the helmet of salvation, the sword of the Spirit (which is the word of God) and prayer—on all occasions and of all kinds—these are our protection but also our motivation. We refuse to look for evil without also seeing that God, throughout history, has adamantly been at work in our cities and communities. Sin, past or present, individual or systemic, doesn't stop us, it provides a way forward—"for the possibility of leaving a chapter of history behind, never to open it again [and] for the possibility to open a chapter that will never close. Patterns may repeat, but never history itself . . ."[55] When the patterns present themselves, we recognize them for what they are and prayerfully work toward institutions—the church included—that heal and serve.

On the bridge of the beautiful Český Krumlov Castle, we bought our two grandsons play swords. They wildly "fenced" their way through ancient streets where knights once bravely protected their city. Along the way, a few misguided "stabs" poked passersby, but the boys didn't notice. Their fight was real. You could see it in their eyes. God has invited us to join the peaceful, real (not play!) fight of our lives. It must hold the reality of a realm we cannot see in either direction. We gauge our progress on the

---

[54] Harvie M. Conn, and Manuel Ortiz, *Urban Ministry : The Kingdom, the City, & the People of God* (Downers Grove, Ill.: InterVarsity Press, 2001). 367.

[55] Paul J. Pastor, *The Face of the Deep: Exploring the Mysterious Person of the Holy Spirit* (Colorado Springs, CO: David C. Cook, 2016). 133.

transformation of people *and* systems, and we fortify our next move with the power of prayer.

Part 2

Hope

The journey of resistance addresses fear from within and without. It brings us to a reality of what is and then, in hope, nudges us forward to hear, see, and feel differently about the possibilities of the gospel, the city . . . and yes, the Church. The push of hope is a present life-giving source of open definitions and viable alternatives revealed in the power of his death and resurrection.

5

Hope for The City: Finding the Good

It is my contention that the city, though plagued with many social
ills and broken on numerous fronts, is still at its core a gift from God. I
would even venture to say it is the result of divine intention.

~ Sean Benesh
View from the Urban Loft: Developing a Theological Framework
for Understanding the City

However, while the Galilean context of Jesus's ministry appears to
be focused on rural communities, it would be a mistake to presume Galilee
was a region untouched by urbanization.

~ Colin Smith
Mind the Gap: Reflections from Luke's Gospel

Ethnic food filled eight-foot long tables end-to-end around the inner
perimeter of a room large enough to hold a couple of hundred people. The
outer perimeter was lined with chairs so the guests could grab a sample plate
of goodies and be seated, but just long enough to devour a taste of heaven
before giving up their chair to the next invitee. This was no "plain vanilla"
celebration. Unique flavors—savory and sweet—mingled with the pleasant,
friendly conversation of Africans, Mexicans, Ukrainians, Eastern Europeans,

Asians, Middle Easterners, and Anglos to make this a truly "international" event. As diverse as the group was, none of the guests traveled more than a few blocks. The dedication of Sunrise Community Center, sponsored by the Rockwood Community Development Corporation, is a center of ministry, business, and training. It is operated by, used by, and accessed by neighbors. "Rockwood is Oregon's poorest community. It is also its sickest [least healthy], most violent, most diverse and least churched community,"[56] but you would not have known that on this day. Instead, there was neighbor with neighbor gathered in an atmosphere of profound hope—people blessed with today's provision, looking forward to a better tomorrow—this was the true *taste of heaven*.

What pleasure God takes in community—in people who find good in the midst of brokenness. God's "good" was established in creation. At every point of His creative *making* of the earth, animals, plants, oceans and rivers, mountains and valleys, the biblical commentary was the same, "And God saw that it was good (Gen 1)." I often assume that if I lived in a garden, I too could declare, "It is good!" That goodness is exponentially more difficult to find—much less declare—in surroundings of abandoned homeless encampments that leave streets or green spaces littered with garbage and human waste; *or* old industrial buildings rusting away against a distant background of snow covered mountains; *or* drug deals going down at local schools; *or* strip clubs flourishing near parks and churches. A focus on the bad comes quite natural--we need a reminder that God and his goodness is alive and well in the city!

Intended for Good

Archeologists and anthropologists continue to make exceptional discoveries as they unearth the ruins of ancient cities. Most agree that the formation of cities evolved as humans moved from hunting and gathering to

---

[56] Rockwood Community Development Corporation, "Rockwood Cdc 2015 Annual Report," https://www.rockwoodcdc.org/wp-content/uploads/2016/01/Rockwood-CDC-Annual-Report-2015.pdf, 2016, accessed April 5, 2016.

farming, to the creation of pottery and metal implements. Finally, an Urban Revolution resulted from advanced agricultural practices, food surplus, and increased societal needs that demanded occupations other than agriculture. These developments eventually led to complex societies, social structures and wars.[57] While there is certainly evidence of both sustainable environment and self-protection as the "precondition" of a city's existence, John Reader is one of the few experts that contends protection may not have played an initial role; and in regard to food supply, "it could have been the other way around . . . the rise of cities [could have] proceeded—and inspired—the intensification of agriculture."[58]

Catal Hüyük, often described as "the world's first city,"[59] gives credence to the theory stated above. A Neolithic Period (ca. 9000-4500 B.C.) settlement in central Turkey, this "city" could be described as "more of an overgrown village than a city—or a town—even though many modern urban centres have far smaller populations."[60] Noting many of the unique features of Catal Hüyük, Reader states:

> A large number of people began living together in permanent houses at a single site. Why? It makes no sense . . . there is nothing at Catal Hüyük to suggest that warfare provoked the development. No less significantly, the rich potential of the surrounding environment could have been more readily exploited by people living in small settlements spread out across the landscape, rather than by thousands packed so closely together at Catal Hüyük. But perhaps the incongruity of people living so closely together that they entered their houses through holes in the roofs, with no apparent benefit in terms of food supply and no need in terms of security, is a clue to how the transition from

---

[57] Thomas V. Brisco, *Holman Bible Atlas* (Nashville, TN: Broadman & Holman, 1998). 35.

[58] Reader. 10.

[59] James Mellaart quoted in John Reader.16.

[60] Ibid. 16.

nomadic hunting and gathering to farming might have affected the minds and worldview of the people involved.[61]

The effects of people living in a densely populated community resulted in the development of a mixed food supply strategy; strong family property rights; products, such as cosmetics, jewelry and mirrors; and numerous artworks, including a painting that is recognized as the "earliest known picture of humanity's presence in an identifiable landscape."[62] This early model of urbanity helps us understand the existence of cities is not just a reaction to conditions of surplus or threats of war (though both are important factors); but may well have been the result of an intentional and desirable common life.

Planned Community

It is no mistake that humankind was created in community and for community. The Father, Son, and Holy Spirit participated in the formation of the world—together and in relationship to one another. From the "good" created by a "Trinitarian circle"[63] of relational ingenuity, men and women were charged with the task of fruitfulness, multiplication, and stewardship of the earth (Gn 1:28). This command, often referred to as the Cultural Mandate, could just as easily be called an "Urban Mandate"[64] to be implemented by humankind with image-bearing creativity. The bedrock of the economic, social, cultural, and architectural constructs of today's cities is the need for community.

If we looked no further, and if we had no deeper understanding of the thick concepts of community and relational living, the Garden is a great start. However, it does not end there. The Apostle John makes it "crystal" clear:

---

[61] Ibid. 18-19.

[62] Ibid. 20.

[63] Stephen A. Seamands, *Ministry in the Image of God : The Trinitarian Shape of Christian Service* (Downers Grove, Ill.: InterVarsity Press, 2005). 12.

[64] Sean Benesh, *View from the Urban Loft: Developing a Framework for Understanding the City* (Eugene, OR: Resource Publications, 2011). 65.

> Then I saw "a new heaven and a new earth,". . . I saw the
> Holy City, the new Jerusalem coming down out of heaven
> from God . . . Then the angel showed me the river of the
> water of life, as clear as crystal, flowing from the throne of
> God and of the Lamb down the middle of the great street of
> the city. . . The throne of God and of the Lamb will be in the
> city, and his servants will serve him. (Rv 21:1, 2; 22:1-3)

Sean Benesh, author of *The Urbanity of the Bible,* quotes Scot McKnight to
bring understanding to these verses:

> God originally placed Adam and Eve in a garden-temple,
> but when God gets things wrapped up, the garden
> disappears. Instead of a garden . . . we find a *city.* The
> garden, in other words, is not the ideal condition. The ideal
> condition is a flourishing, vibrant, culture-seeking, God-
> honoring, Jesus-centered city.[65]

McKnight's description helps us picture God's good *in* and *for* community.
His words lend hope, not just for the city that is coming, but for the city that
is now. The relational paradigm of a city has the potential to ignite creative
genius, lead the way to new discoveries, display the beauty of the arts, solve
the previously unsolvable, reflect Christ's light and mirror God's glory. This
depiction of the city may escape us, but it has never escaped God.

City Potential and Possibility

We are woefully aware that the garden-temple was disrupted by sin.
Yet, even if Adam and Eve had not disobeyed, "the future of humankind
outside the garden was destined to play out in cities."[66] Just as the death and
resurrection of Christ was imminent before the foundations of the world, so
is Christ's second coming, the consummation of his kingdom, and the New
Jerusalem—*his* city. "There is coming a day, when all the layers of smut and

---

[65] Scot McKnight quoted in Benesh, *The Urbanity of the Bible.* 30.
[66] Benesh, *View from the Urban Loft: Developing a Framework for Understanding the City.* 65.

garbage and injustice and blood and exploitation will be burned up and the earth will be *found,* seen for what it *really* is, what God intended it to be all along."[67]

During his time on earth, Jesus saw past the rubble sin had capriciously left in its quake, and he *found* potential and possibility in places most would choose to ignore. Much of his ministry life was spent in Galilee, a region north of Judea, and Capernaum became the home base from which he traveled out to the surrounding area. This strategic fishing city/village was home to many of Christ's miracles and the place where Matthew, Andrew, Peter, James and John were called to follow him.

Capernaum, like so many modern cities, had a reputation and a history. In biblical context, Isaiah's prophetic words repeated in Matthew's gospel tell much of the story.

> Land of Zebulun and the land of Naphtali,
>
> the way of the Sea, beyond the Jordan,
>
> Galilee of the Gentiles—
>
> the people living in darkness have seen a great light;
>
> on those living in the land of the shadow of death a light has
>
> dawned.
>
> (Mt 4:15,16)

At the time of Isaiah's words, the Assyrians had overrun this region of Israel. Its citizens were in constant threat of invasion by the foreign power—living, quite literally, in the shadow of death. The Prophet makes it known, "When God visits [his] people for redemption, [he] comes where the darkness is greatest; where the [people] sit in the shadow of death."[68]

In the time of Christ, Galilee was crisscrossed with trade routes and Capernaum sat on the Via Maris and at the intersection of major highways

---

[67]John Mark Comer, *Garden City: Work, Rest, and the Art of Being Human* (Grand Rapids, MI: Zondervan, 2015). 240.

[68] G. Campbell Morgan, *Studies in the Four Gospels: The Gospel of Matthew* (Old Tappan, N.J.: Fleming H. Revell Company, 1931). 35.

leading to places such as Tyre, Sidon, Damascus, and Jerusalem.[69] Not far from Capernaum, the Romans built influential cities that touched Galilee with "urbanization . . . cities through which the Romans extended political and economic control."[70]

> Sepphoris, Tiberias, and Magdala injected a more pronounced Hellenistic/Roman element into the Galilean ethos. Theaters, palaces, and hippodromes found in larger cities added cultural spice to the mix. Greek could be heard, especially in the cities, along with the more common Aramaic. Even villages like Chroazim and Capernaum could also have non-Jews as residents . . .[71]

Capernaum, it seems, was an energetic, colorful, wannabe urban start-up of a town on the way to everywhere. At the same time, the influences of both the Greeks and Romans never quite let the city or the area outlive the derision of their Jewish neighbors to the south. I imagine, on Judea's part, Galilee, its cities, and its people were *less than*—inferior enough to remain under a questionable shadow of reserved judgment by outsiders.

Jesus saw those living under the stigma of *less than* and fulfilled Isaiah's prophecy to bring Light and Truth. He saw a people poised for redemption and transformation and mission. He saw a city that, disproportionate to its size, would serve as a place, a crossroads, from which his message could spread . . . to all nations. Matthew tells us Jesus "lived in Capernaum" (Mt 4:13) and that it was "his own city" (Mt 9:1 NKJV). The gospel writer, Luke, finds Jesus in *his* city at the synagogue, in homes, and in the streets (Lk 4:31-41). He identified with this city at every point, and nothing could dissuade his compassionate intervention on behalf of its people nor deter his message of hope.

---

[69] G. Campbell Morgan, *Studies in the Four Gospels: The Gospel of Luke* (Old Tappan, N.J.: Fleming H. Revell Company, 1931). 66.

[70] Colin Smith, *Mind the Gap: Reflections from Luke's Gospel on the Divided City* (Portland, OR: Urban Loft Publishers, 2015). 48.

[71] Brisco. 220.

The quirkiness and beauty of "my own city," Portland, has been mentioned. After all, who can resist the home of an Annual Naked Bike Ride or Voodoo Donuts? (As a disclaimer, I have enjoyed many a bacon and cheese covered maple bar at one of the city's most unique donut shops, BUT *fortunately,* I have never been a participant in *or* spectator at the Naked Bike Ride!). Disturbing statistics, however, offset the charm of "Rose City quirky" and its natural beauty. Portland is known as a haven for strip clubs, with more clubs per capita than any U.S. city.[72] Statistical data is difficult to prove, but the reputation is upheld on a short drive through almost any section of the city.

Homelessness, too, is a huge concern for Portland. In fact, HUD (the U.S. Department of Housing and Urban Development) listed Oregon as the state with the highest number of unsheltered people and the highest in unsheltered families with children in 2016.[73] As the largest, most urban city, Portland's streets are home to the majority of those counted in the statewide study. The challenge becomes one of seeing the whole picture in the brightness of God's redeeming light rather than giving up in the face of the brokenness and darkness.

Finding the good in brokenness is an attribute constantly exercised by Christ. Jesus was not unaware of Capernaum's dark side; yet implicit in the darkness was Light that seized the opportunity to cast its rays on God's intent for a place and people. In the many years my husband and I served church planting endeavors, we learned to look at the demographics and potential for success (i.e. numbers and financial assets). Never once did we receive or give training that cast light on the city with the worst reputation or

---

[72] Willamette Week, "Portland Is Still the Strip Club Capital of America, Http://Www.Wweek.Com/Portland/Blog-33364-Portland-Is-Still-the-Strip-Club-Capital-of-America.Html," 2015, accessed February 28, 2017.

[73] OregonLive, "Most of Oregon'a Homeless Live on Street, in Cars, Parks: Highest Percentage in U.S., Says Hud Report, Http://Www.Oregonlive.Com/Trending/2016/11/Homeless_Unsheltered_Oregon_Hu.Html," 2016, accessed February 28, 2017.

the neighborhood with the greatest crime. It's clear, Jesus sees differently than we do. We may be angry at activities that promote evil, despise human exploitation, hate poverty; but in our realistic estimation of *what* is happening, we must assess the city with spiritual mindfulness of the *people* and *places* to which we have been called. They are places and people of hope.

In 2015, my church organization was in the midst of a national "city initiative," aimed at starting new ministries in U.S. world-class cities, such as Atlanta and New York. At a gathering of national leaders in downtown Los Angeles, Tim Keller, pastor of Redeemer Presbyterian Church in New York, addressed the crowd and provided a small booklet entitled *Why God Made Cities*. Keller states:

> Now, why did God invent the city? If we study the Bible, we
> will see many different purposes, but let me give you three.
> All of these purposes are still in effect today, though they
> have been harmed and twisted by sin. But without seeing
> them, you won't understand what the city does and why.
> *God designed the city to release human potential, to shelter*
> *the weak, and to compel spiritual searching.*[74]

Cities are intended by God to be flourishing places of human creativity; they are intended to offer protection; and they are destined as places that ignite the pursuit of God at every level of human existence. These well-stated purposes will unfold as we continue to examine the hope God has for our cities. However, the first step is to see community as a blessing and cities as an extraordinary gift of God.

My City is His City

Jesus, after an incredible day of miracles in Capernaum—including the deliverance of a demon-possessed man (in church, no less!), the healing of Peter's mother-in-law, and multiple healings in the crowd that gathered—

---

[74] Timothy Keller, *Why God Made Cities* (New York: Redeemer City to City, 2013). 11.

made an important statement. As the multitude of healed and delivered tried to keep him from leaving, he said, "I must proclaim the good news of the kingdom of God to the other towns also, because that is why I was sent (Lk 4:43)." It was Christ's mission of hope to proclaim the kingdom in Galilee, among its despised cities, *and* in Judea, where the blessed city of Jerusalem rejected him. Truly his "own city" is *every* city.

Your city, like Portland, has neighborhoods such as Rockwood. They represent the "other"—the neglected places with tragic history or a stigma to overcome. Rockwood, literally located in "The Other Portland" (a pejorative name for the east side of the city), has often been whispered about with contempt. However, the celebration of the Rockwood Sunrise Community Center, a building rescued from the ownership of a strip club "chain," has brought another kind of reputation. The center is developing on-site businesses, job opportunities and training, English language classes, after-school programs, legal aid, space for community activities and church services. A community existing in the shadows has become hopeful once again—just as God intended. Rockwood and Catal Hüyük, separated by millennia, share a Creation old revelation. Can you hear God speak, "Community is good. The *city* is good. Your city is intentional, desirable, full of possibilities to reach the world . . . hopeful."

6

Hope for The Least: Finding Heart

Of all the things God has made, human beings have pride of place in his heart, because they were made in his image (Gen 9:6; James 3:9). Cities, quite literally, have more of the image of God per square inch than any other place on earth. How can we not be drawn to such masses of humanity if we care about the same things God cares about?

~ Timothy J. Keller
Center Church: Doing Balanced, Gospel-Centered Ministry in Your City

These are the least, the last, and the lost, picked up off the streets of the cities by people of faith, who are breathing new life into them. They are loving them into wholeness. They are restoring cities by restoring one person at a time.

~ Barbara J. Elliott
Street Saints: Renewing America's Cities

. . . he rescues the poor at the first sign of need, the destitute who have run out of luck. He opens a place in his heart for the down-and-out, he restores the wretched of the earth. He frees them from tyranny and torture—when

they bleed, he bleeds; when they die, he dies.

~ King Solomon

Psalm 72:13-14 (The Message Bible)

In the mountains just above Los Angeles, I sat before a large stone fireplace in a comfortable lodge-like living room with colleagues. We were discussing modern Gnosticism—not a topic that would come up just anywhere or with anyone. As those who serve our organization at various points of ministry support, a concern was voiced for the growing number of leaders among us "burning out for Jesus." One mentioned a recent conversation in which a pastor stated, "I'll sleep when I get to heaven!" The recognition that our beliefs (rooted or not in our theology) often spawn a vagrant disregard for our humanness and an elevated emphasis of spiritual activity as what truly pleases God.

Ancient Gnosticism has many complexities, but to put it simply, anything material—from the physical realm of the world to our physical bodies—was considered evil. Further, Gnostics believed that there existed "a special, mystical knowledge reserved for those with true understanding. That knowledge was the secret key to salvation."[75] The erroneous teaching deduced that "the world is not our true home, but rather an obstacle to the salvation of the spirit—a view which, although officially rejected by orthodox Christianity, has frequently been part of it."[76]

The regularity of this type of dualistic thinking has found a normalcy in modern thinking—in the way we view life. Our "fireside" conversation uncovered a gnostic-familiar stamp of approval on such practices as the neglect of exercise, sleep, healthy weight, balanced eating, Sabbath rest, and times of solitude—all in the name of "ministry," of course! Gnostic beliefs linger in the concept that the physical needs of humankind (ours or those of

---

[75] González. 70.
[76] Ibid. 71.

our neighbors) are ancillary to the gospel, unnecessary in light of our "exit" from this evil world, and secondary to the heart of God.

There are, however, no secondary concerns. For God's heart wraps around all that is humanity. While believers are ever so careful to give attention to theology and its practice in day to day living (orthodoxy and orthopraxy), it is the "heart" of our faith, our orthopathy, which moves us to *rightly suffer with* others. The practice of loving others because we are so loved, allows us to feel, communicate, and act with right motives—motives rooted in the deep soil of God's affections. His hope for humankind is wholeness—salvation, rescue, deliverance, healing—in spirit and body. If we choose to bifurcate one from the other, a narrow field is created for God's work in the world. Rather than wrap our hearts around humanity with the shared affections of Christ, a tolerance of human suffering sets in that shields us from the grief and pain of the least—those most often overlooked or ignored.

Finding Heart . . . Again

It has been my personal sense that Christ is bringing newfound balance to his church. More often than I care to admit, the dominant Western culture prompts the church in one direction or the other. In one "season" of the early twentieth century, secular opinion held that reason, not spiritual regeneration, would *save* society; therefore, "social ministry" became *everything!* In reaction, a number of believers began to distance themselves from a doctrine that centered itself on works rather than faith, physical wellbeing instead of spiritual rebirth. The renewed emphasis of community involvement in our day—both in secular and church circles—has raised concern that the scale may be tipped too far one direction or the other, depending on who the scale belongs to!

Author Christopher Wright reminds us:

To change people's social or economic status without
leading them to saving faith and obedience to Christ leads
no further than the wilderness or the exile—both places of

death . . . but on the other hand to think that spiritual
evangelism is all there is to mission is to leave people
vulnerable in other ways . . . one can be a Christian on the
way to heaven and make a virtue out of paying little
attention to the physical, material, familial, societal, and
international needs and crises that abound . . . beneath their
noses and under their feet, the poor were uncared for at best
and trampled on at worst. Spiritual religion flourished
amidst social rottenness. And God hated it... Mal 1:10.[77]

This rather strong admonition is meant to get our attention! Whenever the
God of love hates something, it is because it involves people for whom he
gave his life. I John 3:16-18 graciously, but pointedly states:

This is how we know what love is: Jesus Christ laid down his
life for us. And we ought to lay down our lives for our
brothers and sisters. If anyone has material possessions and
sees a brother or sister in need but has no pity on them, how
can the love of God be in that person? Dear children, let us
not love with words or speech but with actions and in truth.

"Vibrant faith should produce a visible outpouring. This is not a theology of
salvation by works. It is a way of taking the temperature of people who claim
to be believers."[78]

The temperature of vibrant faith will find the people of God loving
what and *whom* God loves. His character is manifest in our actions and
finds us spending ourselves on behalf of others. Faith makes us new people
in Christ (II Cor 5:17), ready and willing to obey God's word, proclaim his
message of salvation, and "join him in the work he does, the good work he
has gotten ready for us to do . . . (Eph 2:10, The Message)." The Apostle Paul
in his letter to the Galatians rightly describes this response to a life of faith.

---

[77] Wright. 286-287.
[78] Barbara J. Elliott, *Street Saints : Renewing America's Cities* (Philadelphia:
Templeton Foundation Press, 2004). 264.

He asks, "But what happens when we live God's way (Gal 5:22)?" In a *well-let-me-tell- you* manner he answers his own question:

> He brings gifts into our lives, much the same way that fruit
> appears in an orchard—things like affection for others,
> exuberance about life, serenity. We develop a willingness to
> stick with things, a sense of compassion in the heart, and a
> conviction that a basic holiness permeates things and people
> . . . (Gal 5:23, The Message).

The heart of the gospel and our faith is here. This is the balance that, regardless of church or secular culture, doesn't play to trends. It is a faith that never loses passion for the eternal hope Christ brings to all who believe. It is a faith that opens its heart and life to those among us most in need.

Hope and a Cup of Cold Water (aka Hot Coffee)

Living in Portland has brought me to a couple of grand realizations. This city will not let me ignore the people right "under my feet," as Wright so eloquently states in the quote above. Urban Portland, not to mention the faith community, promotes volunteerism and social action like most cities promote tourism. Secondly, living here has brought the awareness that I am indeed a certifiable, sometimes pretentious, coffee snob. Perhaps both the recognition of people and coffee should be prerequisites of discipleship for every self-respecting Jesus-follower. I'm *slightly* joking about the fetish for good coffee, but seeing people through Christ's eyes—it is essential. Over the course of my time in the city, God has allowed some special encounters to help me understand how he views the least among us. And, for sure, most of them took place over coffee!

A national "breakfast-all-day" restaurant franchise, located down the street from My Father's House Family Shelter, served as a meeting place for volunteer "mentoring" sessions with a lovely homeless mother. Weekly, for close to a year, I drank lots of *inferior* coffee while listening to the story of a woman who had experienced life's worst. *Sarah* (not her real name) was unbelievably optimistic given her past and present circumstances. She and her young son found themselves without resources following Sarah's late in life pregnancy, the death of her mother, and her inability to secure a job. Sarah hoped to find work, aspired to be a good mother, and as a new believer, she wanted to please God. Everything in me wanted to find solutions for this woman. I wanted her life to be different—even more than she did. After weeks of offering sage advice on a variety of topics, praying with her, and offering encouragement at the smallest steps forward, I had an incredible revelation: Sarah was not a project. I was not the savior. Well-known priest and author, Henri Nouwen stated:

> We are not the healers, we are not the reconcilers, we are
> not the givers of life. We are sinful, broken, vulnerable
> people who need as much care as anyone we care for. The
> mystery of ministry is that we have been chosen to make our
> own limited and very conditional love the gateway for the
> unlimited and unconditional love of God. Therefore, true
> ministry must be mutual.[79]

I needed Sarah as much, maybe more than she needed me. The vulnerability and insecurities of my own life came to the surface as, friend to friend, we laughed and cried. I dispensed plenty of advice, but Sarah's wisdom, her street smarts, her management of a miniscule income, and her creativity made for an active, real, and mutual friendship. If I gave her a "cup of cold water (Mt 10:42)"—or bad coffee—it compared little to the buckets of blessing I received from a single mother with nothing to her name.

Across town from the homeless shelter, Brother Bruce (his street name!) invited my husband and I to accompany him on one of his routine "rounds" of early morning coffee delivery under the Morrison Street Bridge. A few instructions were offered: Don't wake people. Do engage them in conversation. Be willing to shake hands. Above all, look them in the eye.

---

[79] Henri Nouwen quoted in Elliott, *Street Saints: Renewing America's Cities*, 257.

Watching Bruce in action was fascinating. He knew many by name. He would gently crouch down and speak in low tones to the rumpled, unwashed, blurry-eyed men and women who had just spent a wet, cold night in a sleeping bag or under a tarp. "Would you like a cup of coffee? Hot chocolate? How about a banana or granola bar?" Simple questions often opened the door for deep conversations and Bruce was willing, resting on his "haunches," to take the time to listen. Occasionally, someone would request prayer. Some would ask for money. Some didn't want to be bothered, but most were grateful for morning coffee delivered to their "door" with kindness.

Brother Bruce, educated and ordained, put his training aside to meet people in desperate circumstances. He seemed to instinctively know what they needed, often providing critical shelter information or how to obtain needed medicine. So as we carried hot pots of coffee and morning treats like stadium food vendors, we watched humility, compassion, grace, and love in action. These were our lessons, our blessing for the day. The teacher, Brother Bruce, was God's hand extending a cup of cold water, but the real instructors were disguised as recipients of charity. They were people of the streets who, in an almost eerie way, reflected my own human longings for kindness and love. They mirrored my dependence on others for the things in life I'm privileged to enjoy. Greater still, they served as a representation of God's unconditional love for humankind—the same unrestricted, unqualified grace that sustains at every point of my own weakness and suffering.

Hope, Sheep, and Goats

To sear our hearts with the importance of the homeless, the poor, the imprisoned, and the hungry, Jesus tells his disciples a story about his return and rule—his consummated kingdom. It entails the Son of God separating the goats from the sheep in much the same way as a shepherd. This act of separating the righteous and the unrighteous may not be for the reasons we would think. Author Laurie Beshore sheds this light on the parable:

> The factor that determines how the sheep are separated has nothing to do with our human measurements for success. Jesus doesn't separate people based on their worldly achievements, their personality traits, or their record of church attendance. The deal breaker is whether they cared for those in need. Those who served the poor are invited into heaven, while those who didn't are sent away.[80]

As the story unfolds, not only do we find the "deal breaker" astounding, but we also discover why the least *are* the primary factor.

Jesus addresses the sheep, "Come . . . for I was hungry and you gave me something to eat, I was thirsty and you gave me something to drink, I was a stranger and you invited me in, I needed clothes and you clothed me, I was in prison and you came to visit me (Mt 25:34-36)." The sheep are perplexed and question, "Lord, when did we see you hungry and feed you, or thirsty and give you something to drink? When did we see you a stranger and invite you in, or needing clothes and clothe you? When did we visit you in prison (vs. 37-39)?" These precious individuals may very well have been waiting for Jesus to clarify his mistake: "Umm . . . there's been a mix up. You must not be the right ones! Just step over to my left with the goats!" (A bit reminiscent of the 2017 Oscars: The winner is *La La Land*! Oops! It's actually *Moonlight!*)

Of course, Jesus did not make such a comment. He explained the unimaginable, "Whatever you did for the least of these brothers and sisters of mine, you did it for me (vs. 40)." When they encountered "the least," they encountered Jesus. When they cared and served, they were caring for and serving Christ. The acts came so naturally—an innate response of the Spirit

---

[80] Laurie Beshore, *Love without Walls : Learning to Be a Church in the World for the World* (Grand Rapids, MI: Zondervan, 2012). 23.

and character of Christ within—they had no idea of the kingdom impact. Beshore states:

> [T]he actions that Jesus refers to in this parable seem so small and insignificant that the people chosen to enter heaven cannot identify anything special they had done to draw God's attention. They engaged in these simple acts out of the overflowing of their love for Jesus, yet they had eternal consequences, consequences that affect the one who gives far more than the one who receives.[81]

Christopher Heuertz and Christine Pohl in their book, *Friendships at the Margins,* go in depth on our critical need for the "prophetic presence of friends who are poor" to grace, enrich, and complete our lives.[82] In reference to Matthew twenty-five, they comment:

> If we see that care for persons in need is a response of love to Jesus, . . . a chance to walk on holy ground, then our entire understanding of mission and ministry shifts. It is not what "we" do for "them," but an opportunity for all of us to be enveloped in God's grace and mercy. In God's economy, it's less clear who is donor and who is recipient because all are blessed when needs are met and when individuals receive care.[83]

The consequences of our actions, or lack thereof, are eternal, but they are initiated in the present. In real time, every cup of water given to the thirsty, every piece of bread or clothing, every act of hospitality, every visit to the overlooked or ignored is reciprocated with the presence of Christ. Every act of mercy neglected is the absence of a blessing.

---

[81] Ibid. 24.
[82] Christopher L. Heuertz, and Christine D. Pohl, *Friendship at the Margins : Discovering Mutuality in Service and Mission, Resources for Reconciliation* (Downers Grove, IL: IVP Books, 2010). 76.
[83] Ibid. 77.

Sheltering the Least

Cities are points of protection and shelter, hope for many who would otherwise be overlooked. The homeless flock to inner cities where services are readily available—at least in theory. Refugees are relocated in cities or communities needing more than a place to stay, but also friendship and acclamation to a new culture. Inmates in jails and prisons are "sheltered" with four walls and a roof, but are in constant need of protection from paralyzing loneliness, physical and emotional violence, and survival skills for real life when they are released. Whether the urban core in a major city or a town receiving the overflow of urban crisis, protection for the most vulnerable remains a primary function of society—and a high priority for Christ's church.

Serving the spiritual and physical needs of the poor was not a conflict for the early church. The gospel was "fully preached" (Rom 15:19 NKJV) producing faith communities full of men and women who *believed* and *lived* that gospel in the cities of the then-known world.[84]

Sociologist Rodney Stark confirms:

Christianity revitalized life in Greco-Roman cities by providing new norms and new kinds of social relationships able to cope with many urgent and urban problems. To cities filled with the homeless and impoverished, Christianity provided a new and expanded sense of family. To cities torn by violence and ethnic strife, Christianity offered a new basis for social solidarity. And to cities faced with epidemics, fires, and earthquakes, Christianity offered effective nursing services.[85]

---

[84] Lesslie Newbigin, *The Gospel in a Pluralist Society* (Grand Rapids, Mich.,Geneva SZ: W.B. Eerdmans ; WCC Publications, 1989). 120-121.

[85] Rodney Stark, *The Rise of Christianity: A Sociologist Reconciles History* (Princeton, N.J.: Princeton University Press, 1996). Quoted in Corbett and Fikkert. 44.

Christ had laid claim to the whole of believers' lives, and as they found themselves in close proximity to the need, they set aside personal comfort to extend his grace and mercy to every aspect of those "in need."

Mercy contains and communicates the gospel—good news for body and spirit—but the wholeness of the message has never gone unchallenged. When the organized church came on the scene, "Acts of Corporal Mercy," urged Christians to feed the hungry, give water to the thirsty, clothe the naked, shelter the homeless, visit the sick, visit those in prison, and bury the dead. "Acts of Spiritual Mercy" were also incorporated. They included such activities as prayer, admonishment, instruction, counsel, forgiveness, consolation, and patience.[86] These two sets of values were no doubt recognition of the holistic need in humankind, yet some of the latter were reserved for priests alone. This intimated that certain acts of mercy were of greater importance, and that material or physical acts of mercy were *other than spiritual*. Notwithstanding a hint of dualism, the acts of mercy, with slight variations, were intricate to discipleship and worship in the Catholic Church and in future movements such as Methodism.

John Wesley, the founder of the Methodist Church, was known for visiting the sick and imprisoned, speaking out against slavery, and giving his finances to the poor. Rev. Steven Manskar, quoted in a current Methodist publication, states:

> An important piece that is frequently missed when we discuss works of mercy today is that Wesley believed Christians must also care for the spiritual needs of people... For Wesley, evangelism, proclaiming the good news of Jesus Christ, his forgiveness of sin and love for all people— especially the poor, marginalized and oppressed—is as much a work of mercy as is feeding the hungry.[87]

---

[86] Catholic Encyclopedia New Advent, Acts of Corporal and Spiritual Mercy, "Http://Www.Newadvent.Org/Cathen/10198d.Htm," accessed March 29, 2017.

[87] Interpreter Magazine "Means of Grace-Offering Mercy Interpreter Magazine, Receiving Grace", "Http://Www.Interpretermagazine.Org/Topics/Means-of-Grace-Offering-Mercy-Receiving-Grace#Main," accessed March 28, 2017.

"Proclaiming good news is as much a work of mercy as feeding the hungry." Those are important words, because if we understand the heart of what Wesley believed, we also know that the converse is true: Feeding the hungry is as much a work of mercy as evangelism. Both are "spiritual." Both are kingdom focused and together represent a gospel fully preached. Heuertz and Pohl remind us:

> Human beings who are not Christians are far more than potential converts. In our concern for reaching out with the gospel, we can unwittingly reduce the person to less than the whole being that God formed. When we shrink our interest in people to the possibilities of where their souls may spend eternity, it is easy to miss how God might already be working **in** and **through** a particular person.[88] (Emphasis mine)

God's present work *in* a person is often invisible—sometimes unknown to the person herself or himself. His work *through* a person toward others can just as easily be missed. How often have we been somewhere "in space" when Jesus asked us for a place to sleep or a hot meal!

Hope for the vulnerable, in essence, holds hope for the church and for every Christ- follower. These are a gift to us, testing the metal of our faith, challenging us to keep the pieces of humanity stitched together. The gospel is a balanced representation of God's heart: He sent his Son to suffer and die (physically), so we could be forgiven, delivered, healed in spirit AND body, in mind and emotion. Our *orthopathy* can be an expression of both our orthodoxy and orthopraxy. We still believe Christ is the One and Only Savior of the world. We hold tight to evangelism as an urgent task for the church. But, we also rightly suffer with others—feel what they feel—"crouch" to speak words of mercy and hand a cup of steaming coffee on a cold morning—because in doing so, we give and then receive a longed-for completeness, wholeness. We find ourselves broken before the broken,

---

[88] Heuertz, and Pohl. 30-31.

humbled by the wisdom of the weak, inspired by the creativity of those with few resources; and most amazingly, energized by what our small contribution can accomplish when empowered by the Spirit, present and at work. Finding God's heart is finding a heart for the least. It already beats in us. His "heart" causes us to care for the same things he cares for, enables us to restore cities by restoring one person at a time, and prompts us to rescue the poor at the first sign of need. That is who we are. That is what we do.

7

Hope for The Last: Finding Innocence

So I'd say my philosophy isn't just about mending bodies. It's about restoring people's independence, giving them a life, not just an existence. It's about respect and love and dignity. Those are the things we owe our children. Children are the ones who need them most of all.

~ Christina Noble
Mama Tina: The Christina Nobel Story Continues

The spirit that receives a child and will not offend it, is the spirit that will not put a stumbling-block in the way of the world. The man [or woman] who offends a child is the man [or woman] who offends the world."

~ G. Campbell Morgan
The Gospel of Matthew

What do you think? If a man owns a hundred sheep, and one of them wanders away, will he not leave the ninety-nine on the hills and go to look for the one that wandered off? . . . In the same way your Father in heaven is not willing that any of these little ones should perish.

Matthew 18:12, 14

The historic Mississippi District in urban Portland is home to DeNorval Unthank Park, formerly Kerby Park, renamed and dedicated in 1969 to the city's first African American doctor. Decades previous, in 1929, Unthank had been recruited because the city *needed* a black doctor. He moved west and bought a home in the prestigious white neighborhood of Westmoreland, only to face harassment from neighbors. Escalated threats and vandalism increased to the point it was necessary to find a safer neighborhood in which his family could reside. After several moves, the Unthanks became residents of the Irvington neighborhood, less than two miles from the old Kerby Park. Settling into Portland life had not been easy. At a time when black patients were not allowed treatment in Portland's hospitals, Unthank made himself available for house calls, day or night, to African Americans, Asians . . . and many whites as well.[89] In addition to sacrificial care for his patients, Unthank quite naturally became a leading advocate for civil rights. The doctor made an incredible contribution to Portland's black population, city government, and the founding of Portland's NAACP. As the city grew and changed, the once safe "Unthank Park" became gang territory and marred the park's commemorative intent with drugs and violence.[90]

The story, however, does not end in gang violence. The beautiful park that "remembered" a great man for his belief that his city could be a better, less threatening place for future generations, is the present site of Self Enhancement Inc. (SEI),[91] a nonprofit organization that supports underprivileged youth. Tony Hopson, Sr. began SEI in 1981, holding summer camps for high school boys. A member of the community, Tony wanted to find a way to "give back." By 1997, a facility housing a gym, library, auditorium, and classrooms was constructed on a portion of

---

[89] The Oregon Encyclopedia, "Denorval Unthank," https://oregonencyclopedia.org/articles/unthank_denorval_1899_1977 , accessed April 30, 2017.
[90] OregonLive, "North Portland's Untahnk Park Is Rededicated," 2011, accessed May 1, 2017.
[91] Inc. Self Enhancement, "This Is Our Story," https://www.selfenhancement.org/history, accessed April 30, 2017.

Unthank Park to bring a multitude of services to local schools and families. With concerted effort, SEI is raising the level of education and the percentage of graduates by providing a gathering place, in-school coordinators for academic guidance, and after-school programs to expose students to the arts, music, dance, and culture.

The history of the area, the park and its founder, and even the story of SEI came to my attention through a friend who pastors a church in the vicinity. I was aware that Mary Merriweather and her husband, George, were deeply involved with the school system and police to work against gang violence, mentor youth, and support parents—but the depth of that commitment did not "hit home" until I walked the "turf" with Mary. Her intimate relationship as an SEI volunteer and employee offered a view of the heart of an organization that exists to bring hope to the young people in their community.

The mentors and coordinators of this public non-profit provide the fuel necessary to see kids succeed in life and school. These significant adults believe wholeheartedly that it is their job to find and nurture the gift in every child. Not surprisingly, most of the staff members at SEI are professing Christians who, like Mary, felt an undeniable call to serve her community. She and her friends at the center believe the way they follow Christ opens doors to speak about their faith; but it is the practical service and unconditional love that provides the evidence. They proudly hail the unofficial motto of SEI: "Every kid bears our last name!"

The concern and affection, expressed by the above mantra, speaks loudly to the responsibility the adults of any given community hold in the nurture and development of the next generation. Just as strongly, it suggests that there is a greater purpose than simply keeping kids off the streets. These young people represent the hope of a heavenly Father for all his children—young and old—and are the embodiment of Christ to the world. They bear more than his name. They bear his image.

Jesus, Kids, and Surprising Lessons

The Jewish community, much like today, had developed attitudes toward the younger population. Children were considered a blessing. The Torah commanded parents to love, discipline, and teach their children in the ways of God. At the same time, however, these little ones were also among the most powerless in society—they simply had no status apart from their parents.[92] Perhaps that is why author H. Spees notes that when CCCT (Christ-centered Community Transformation) practitioners define the least, last, and the lost, children and youth are identified as the *last* because they are "powerless in our society, voiceless, those who have no vote."[93] Quite opposite to traditional thought, Jesus reinforced children as *chief* among humankind—central to kingdom activity and likeness.

The gospel writer, Matthew, helps us appreciate Christ's view of children and the role they play in adult discipleship by masterfully unfolding a conversation between Jesus and his disciples. The conversation began with a question—something Jesus always welcomed, whether from friend or foe. And he always answered, but often in a way that addressed several deep issues at once—until the original question became rather incidental. (Jesus was a bit radical in that way. The Anointed One of God had a subversive side!) As inquiries were being made among the disciples of "Who, then, is the greatest in the Kingdom of Heaven," Jesus answered with a living illustration and some rather astonishing lessons.

This account found in Matthew 18 needs a bit of backstory for us to fully understand. At first, it appears the disciples are power hungry and full of hubris. After all, we do see a level of self-interest in other passages (i.e. James and John arguing over who will get to sit at Jesus' right hand when he comes into his kingdom). Here, however, the inquiry is posed after Jesus's revelation that he, the Messiah, the Son of God, the King of Kings would "be

---

[92] Craig S. Keener, and InterVarsity Press., *The Ivp Bible Background Commentary : New Testament* (Downers Grove, Ill.: InterVarsity Press, 1993).

[93] Randy White and H Spees, *Out of Nazareth: Christ-Centered Civic Transformation* (Skyforest, CA: Urban Loft, 2017). 54.

delivered into the hands of men. They [would] kill him, and on the third day he [would] be raised to life (Mt 16:21, 17:22-23)." The disciples' minds swirled: This was far from the typical road to power and success! Whatever worldly grandeur of political and religious control they had imagined possible, those mental pictures were slowly displaced. Thus, the question, "Who, *then,* is the greatest in this completely foreign, very strange kingdom of yours where the Leader dies in the process? What kind of kingdom is this anyway? And, what-the-heck kind of person gets the corner office in this reality?" (I took a few liberties with the actual dialogue!) The question really wasn't *who* would be the greatest, but *how* could anyone be great in such a revolutionary kingdom based on self-sacrifice, suffering, and the sheer power of love.

It just so happened the perfect person for this position of greatness was close at hand. Jesus called the small child to come and sit in the center of the group of disciples. I imagine a little boy wearing a grass-stained tunic, a smudge of dirt on his cheek, and a cool stick in hand that doubled as a fishing pole or a sword. The little boy, for all we know, may have been an angelic child, intently listening from the periphery as Christ addressed the crowd; but somehow that seems to defeat the illustration about to unfold as Jesus calls him close and seats him in the midst of the disciples. The stage was set and Jesus spoke,

> Truly I tell you, unless you change and become like little
> children, you will never enter the kingdom of heaven.
> Therefore, whoever takes the lowly position of this child is
> the greatest in the kingdom of heaven. And whoever
> welcomes one such child in my name welcomes me. (Mt
> 18:3-5)

The present and future Kingdom where Christ reigns sovereign touts the innocence of a child as heaven's standard, and the welcome of a child as acceptance of the King.

Welcome and Warning

Jesus redefined greatness, not in terms of high positions held by the powerful or elite, but in the lowly, humble position of a child—not in terms of first place, but last. In their powerless condition, children demonstrate humility in the utter lack of sophistication, unmitigated joy, freedom of expression, simplicity of thought and action, and the infinite pliancy with which they learn. Jesus must have had an intense look in his eyes as he addressed the disciples with a clear requirement, "Unless you change and become like little children . . . there will be no need to worry about greatness in the kingdom of heaven, for without childlike humility and innocence there will be no entrance in the first place (Mt 18:3, Author's paraphrase)!"

The issue of "greatness" had been addressed. The kingdom leadership lessons from one simple show-and-tell illustration were many, but Jesus dove still deeper into just how this unconventional, radical kingdom functioned differently from the worldly governance with which the disciples had been conditioned. Jesus added, with the little one most likely fidgeting in their midst, "Whoever welcomes one such child in my name welcomes me (Mt 18:5)." Not only must the disciples be *like* children, they must *welcome* children. In much the same way as serving the least with food, drink, clothing, and visitation, Jesus again identifies the powerless and vulnerable as embodied representatives of himself.

The gravity might have escaped the disciples were it not for the stern warning and admonishment that followed:

> If anyone causes one of these little ones—those who believe
> in me—to stumble, it would be better for them to have a
> large millstone hung around their neck and to be drowned
> in the depths of the sea . . . woe to the person through whom
> they come . . . if your hand or foot causes you to stumble, cut
> it off and throw it away. It is better for you to enter life
> maimed or crippled than to have two hands or two feet and
> be thrown into eternal fire . . . see that you do not despise

one of these little ones. For I tell you that their angels in
heaven always see the face of my Father in heaven. (Mt. 18:
6-10)

Jesus's horrifying statements must have widened a few eyes and caused a
few mouths to gape open. Millstones were huge—death by drowning certain,
but that may have been preferable to the removal of body parts! Theologian
G. Campbell Morgan illuminates Christ's severe words by lending this
paraphrase of the passage: The "man [or woman] who causes the stumbling
block, becomes a stumbling block to himself [or herself] and if we destroy a
child, we destroy ourselves."[94] And, finally, Jesus cautions, "Do not despise
one of these little ones." The master wanted his disciples to understand that
children were worthy of notice, consideration, and respect. To think little or
nothing of a child is to think little or nothing of Christ or the Father whose
face do angels, on every child's behalf, relentlessly view.

The angels, no doubt, "read" in the Father's face a tender care, love,
and compassion for the little ones they watch over. When it comes to
children, there is great tenderness in God's countenance, but too often, there
is thunder toward those who would think so little of a child as to bring him
or her harm. His gaze does not miss the terrified child placed at the center of
an over-occupied boat of refugees crossing rough waters, or the countless
ten to twelve year-olds exploited in the sex slave industry, or those subjected
to regular abuse by a family member or supposed friend, or the child living
in a war zone, or kids living with the multi-faceted effects of profound
poverty. For those who love Christ, to think little or nothing about children
suffering in such ways is reprehensible.

Full Attention, Sacrificial Love

The Father is ever attentive to *all* little ones--those in our families,
churches, and communities. Children are of great importance in the
kingdom and, therefore, must be a priority to adult leaders and disciples.

---

[94] Morgan, "Studies in the Four Gospels: The Gospel of Matthew." 229.

Having heard more than my fair share of sermons on the Matthew 18 passage, I have finally come to grips with the weightier message Jesus was communicating: Kingdom leadership (greatness) is not possible for anyone who does not receive, welcome, respect, lead, train, and nurture children.

Recently, Natalie Werking, a children's pastor from Indiana, addressed the convention body of my church organization. Using the above verses, she asked us to "think broader about the Great Commission . . . to, yes, reach out to unreached people groups and nations, but also to bend down and say yes to those who are smaller than us, but of great value to the Lord."[95] Our faces should be turning toward, not away, from kids. So strong are the words of Matthew 18, it may not be going too far to say that every believer, every leader in the Body of Christ is called to "Children's Ministry!" If that stretches beyond an exegetical reading of Scripture, one thing is certain from this passage: Children are worthy of our full attention.

The notice and care of children brings hope for God's "now" kingdom to invade the space of our everyday lives. During my graduate studies, I interviewed an individual who has, largely behind the scenes, orchestrated a partnership between city and the church as a means to transform the city of Portland. This man has successfully managed to navigate a river of differences to serve the common good. Seemingly, he has his hand on the pulse of every major issue the city faces. I asked Kevin Palau, "If you could only affect one of the many aspects of social need in our community, what would it be? Where would you begin?" Without hesitation, he replied, "The schools. This is where every major need in society converges."[96] Kevin went on to explain that children are the most affected by poverty, inequitable educational opportunities, addictions, abuse, gun violence, racial or religious prejudices, human trafficking . . . and if we can make a change for them there is hope for the city's future.

---

[95] Natalie Werking, *Reaching Kids in the Community, Commissioned by Jesus* (Washington, D.C.: 2017).
[96] Kevin Palau, ((Interview by author, Portland, OR, October 18, 2011).

Making a change for kids and our communities necessitates a sacrifice on our part, but it also invigorates the child-like innocence of adult hearts to believe they can make a difference. Natalie, mentioned above, and her church were invited by a local school principle to teach kids the values they needed to survive in today's world. The beleaguered public-school principle confided to a local city leader the tremendous number of kids affected by poverty, drugs, and lack of parental guidance. The teachers, already overwhelmed with responsibilities, had little time to instill values, so the troubled students repeatedly ended up in the Principal's office. The city official suggested he call Natalie's church. The church responded by starting an after-school program to teach values based on biblical character traits. The program required extra finances from the church budget, additional staff, and lots and lots of volunteers—but it was worth it. Since the program's inception, the number of "Principal's office" visits have dropped from over six hundred a year to ninety-five a year. Other schools in their community are, to no surprise, asking the church for help![97]

Let's pray we are asked to not just to give money, teach Sunday school, work in the nursery, or participate in a community outreach; but also to love and value kids with the sacrificial love of Christ. Our "greatness" (at least in kingdom dynamics!) hinges on extending a welcome to these who bear his name, reflect his likeness, and have his full attention. In other words, they have his heart. As if to make sure his disciples, then and now, carried that same heart resident within, Jesus softened the thunderous message with the tender story of the lost sheep.

> What do you think? If a man owns a hundred sheep, and
> one of them wanders away, will he not leave the ninety-nine
> on the hills and go to look for the one that wandered off?
> And if he finds it, truly I tell you, he is happier about that
> one sheep than the ninety-nine that did not wander off. In

---

[97] Werking.

101

the same way your Father in heaven is not willing that any of these little ones should perish. (Mt 18:12-14)

Though many have equated the story with a "lost soul" or a believer who has wandered from the faith, G. Campbell Morgan adamantly declares, "[Jesus] was *still talking about a child,* so that another reason we are not to despise a child, is the fact that He has come to find the little child (emphasis mine)."[98] We may take liberties with the application of these verses—for all of us are his sheep and all of us are his children—but in the context these words were spoken, Christ' emphasis was on the child, and he is not willing that any should be lost or perish. Don't despise. Don't offend. Look for the one. Welcome all.

As I close this chapter, I am viewing a picture sent to me by my sister who serves as the Lifestage Pastor at a large church in Hawaii. Lynn oversees the department leaders that serve children, birth through college. Recently, as she was making her "rounds" during the first of three consecutive Sunday morning services, she peeked into children's church to see how things were going. In what was probably a "once in a lifetime occurrence" for this thriving church, there was just one child in attendance. A precious little Hawaiian girl sat alone, dead center in the front row of an otherwise empty room. Standing directly in front of her, Teacher Steve, storyboard at hand, was delivering a Bible lesson with passion. Lynn snapped a quick pic with her iPhone to remind herself and others of the importance Jesus (and Steve!) places on one single child.

Embracing the kingdom's value for every child comes as we embrace our own powerlessness. We can only give children a place in the kingdom when we forsake the sophistication of adulthood for the childlike joy found in simple activities and simple truths. When we begin to grasp this radical kingdom that Jesus leads—where the first are last and the last are first—kids from Portland's Mississippi District, kids from New Castle, kids from Hilo and the cities of the world will be present and accounted for. Hope will

---

[98] Morgan, "Studies in the Four Gospels: The Gospel of Matthew." 231.

resound from the street corner to the corners of the world. All of us will revel in the freedom of newfound innocence. It is time for the adult church to "bend a knee!"[99]

---

[99] Werking.

8

Hope for The Lost: Finding Joy

All authority in heaven and on earth has been given to me. Therefore go and make disciples of all nations, baptizing them in the name of the Father and of the Son and of the Holy Spirit, and teaching them to obey everything I have commanded you. And surely I am with you always, to the very end of the age.

Matthew 28:17b-20

And salvation only does what it's meant to do when those who have been saved, are being saved, and will one day fully be saved realize that they are saved not as souls but as wholes and not for themselves alone but for what God so longs to do through them.

~ N.T. Wright

Surprised by Hope

"'. . . Love the Lord your God with all your heart and with all your soul and with all your mind.' This is the first and greatest commandment. And the second is like it: 'Love your neighbor as yourself . . .'"

Matthew 22:37-39

We saw it, we heard it, and now we're telling you so you can experience it along with us, this experience of communion with the Father and his Son, Jesus Christ. Our motive for writing is simply this: We want you to enjoy this, too. Your joy will double our joy.

I John 1:3-4

Through the good work he inspires in us, we offer every person the opportunity to see the living Christ. Freed from following a formula or script, we share the good news incarnationally, following his pattern, representing his powerful presence, knowing that he is enfleshing himself in and with us in every relationship, every encounter: "I am with you always."

~ H. Spees
Out of Nazareth: Christ-Centered Community Transformation

The seventies era was, for lack of a better term, a tumultuous season in American history. At the tail end of sixties riots and the hippie movement, the new decade gave way to the Kent State anti-war rally, the women's fight for the ERA (Equal Rights Amendment), the Watergate scandal, and the move toward environmental concern after the nuclear meltdown at Three Mile Island. The disillusionment, disappointment, mistrust of government, and outright fear caused by such events had an interesting effect on many churches. There was a definite rise in political involvement and influence as an attempt to preserve traditional values, but there was also a growing belief that Christ's return was imminent—especially with the fresh surge of the Holy Spirit resulting in the conversion of a multitude of young people from the hippie movement. The *real* possibility he could come *today* convinced much of the Christian population at the time that the Great Commission simply could not wait!

The church I was privileged to belong to, as a young teen in the early seventies, was passionate about reaching the lost. Each year the congregation gave thousands of dollars to missions, and we were taught to be faithful witnesses at school, work and in our neighborhoods. The youth were often sent out two by two (so Scriptural!) to canvas the mall or apartment buildings armed with Four Spiritual Laws tracks— pamphlets containing a short gospel message—and a semi-memorized speech, just in case someone actually listened! Participating in the world of Christian "service" was new to me, primarily because I had just been "found" myself. So great was the stress, I actually prayed (well, hoped!) no one would stop as we held out our little tracks for the taking, or that no one would answer when we knocked on a door.

Against All Odds

Thankfully, for me, God did give opportunity for conversation, and he did open doors. I say, "Thankfully for me," because I'm not sure how much good I did the recipients of my message! The good came in my exposure, at a young age, to the simple yet profound fact that God did indeed care about *all* people. The Jesus I was getting to know would go *anywhere* or do *anything* necessary to find lost people, regardless of how hopeless they appeared to be in human eyes. As we entered sub-standard buildings—most likely drug houses, we encountered people who were the definition of "lost"—body, mind, and spirit. On the other side of doors facing dingy halls, often smelly and littered, were faces of addiction and desperation. For sure, I was not from a wealthy or perfect family—we had our issues—but never had I seen people live this way. It wasn't the lack of material goods alone that made them poor, it was the lack of all things essential to human flourishing—love, dignity, and joy.

Whenever I think back on those radical "Jesus people" days, I'm reminded that, though I was timid to share my faith with others, I believed there was an urgency to do so. Most of the church believed it too. The theme of Jesus's quick return was present in sermons, songs, and even musicals. With the refrain of Larry Norman's "I Wish We'd All Been Ready" ringing in our ears, the adult church would rejoice with the youth at how many "received Christ"—those who had an initial interest and cared enough to pray with strangers. We all rejoiced together in a little mini-celebration of applause and hallelujahs. In some ways, we might need to regain the passion and the joy of that era—well, minus the tracks, formulas, and minor manipulation!

Jesus's passion for the lost has never faded. Scripture expresses a present urgency for the task and an undeniable joy in "found-ness." Our human-based enthusiasm can wane when we view people as not just lost but as a lost cause—unrecoverable. The gospel writer, Luke, records a triad of stories or parables that reveal the tenacity, sacrifice and unconditional love of Christ's unstoppable search and rescue efforts. And while the stories speak to the Savior's heart, at the same time they cut deep into what has become, for many Western Christians, a sense of futile duty rather than the joy of discipleship.

Bring on the Party!

Luke opens the account by describing the mixed crowd listening that day. Tax collectors and sinners were gathered along with Pharisees and the teachers of the law. The Pharisees were not too happy about the colorful following. They complained among themselves, "*This* man welcomes sinners and eats with them (Lk 15:2, emphasis mine)." There was, among these religious leaders, a duty to the law that fostered superiority, protectionism, and prejudice. Those whom they saw as the scum of the earth, Jesus saw as friends worthy of celebrating. The narrow view of God's heart and mission echoed in the grumbling of religious leaders prompts the parables that follow. Referred to by one theologian as the "Party Parables,"[100] each end in uncontainable joy that cannot be satisfied to the fullest until it is shared with friends and neighbors.

---

[100] Robert Capon quoted in Smith. 76.

Jesus began with familiar words. Essentially, it is the same story of Matthew 18, and again, the owner of hundred sheep will leave the ninety-nine to find the one that has wandered away. The "Father . . . is not willing that any of these little ones should perish (Mt 18:14)." In the latter telling, Jesus offers a new application. The Shepherd, indicative of Christ himself, puts his own life on the line to rescue the sheep that has strayed into dangerous territory. "When he finds it, he *joyfully* puts it on his shoulders, and goes home (Lk 15:5, 6)." Returning with the sheep, the Shepherd makes a few quick "phone calls" to friends and neighbors for an impromptu party—he couldn't wait to share the joy of the rescue.

Jesus expressed the joy felt in this way: "I tell you that in the same way there will be more rejoicing in heaven over one sinner who repents than over ninety-nine righteous persons who do not need to repent (Lk 15:7)." Some present struggled; for the picture offered was quite remarkable. The Shepherd did not scold sheep number one-hundred. He did not murmur under his breath how much trouble—not to mention risk—the sheep had caused him. Instead, he draped the wayward animal across his shoulders; his wooly coat next to the Shepherds neck, his frightened face next to the Shepherds cheek, and his legs firmly held, two each in the leathered hands of the Shepherd. The joyous party that ensued was a consequence of such grace and love—the kind made possible by the sacrifice and suffering of a Good Shepherd.

Sacrifice and suffering are very often inherent factors of a diligent search. The pursuit is intentional, concerted, and *must* be satisfied. In the second of the three parables, it is with such tenacity that a woman seeks a lost coin. Oil lamp lit and broom in hand, she sweeps her dirt floor, looking under every piece of furniture and in every dark corner until it is found. Her resolve is based in a singular fact: the coin has value but cannot be redeemed unless it is found. Her efforts are rewarded. As soon as the coin was discovered, she calls on friends and neighbors to rejoice for her. With much the same Spirit of delight, Jesus declares, ". . . there is rejoicing in the presence of the angels of God over one sinner who repents (Lk 15:10)." This is a joy that refuses denial.

Finally, Jesus brought the parables to a climax with the story of the lost, or prodigal, son. While the previous stories have a symbolic quality, the last is clearly human, stirring emotions of anguish, disgust, judgment, anger, jealously . . . and wonder. The crowd no doubt marveled as Jesus unveiled the captivating tale of a father willing, at the request of a self-absorbent and rebellious son, to grant an early inheritance. The young man gladly takes the money, leaves for a far-away place, and quickly squanders his fortune on fast living. Coming to the end of his resources, homeless and starving, he takes a job feeding pigs—not the kind of work a Jewish boy puts on his LinkedIn profile! It isn't until the pods he's feeding the pigs start to look appetizing that he comes to his senses:

> ". . . How many of my father's hired servants have food to spare, and here I am starving to death! I will set out and go back to my father and say to him: Father I have sinned against heaven and against you. I am no longer worthy to be called your son; make me like one of your hired servants (Lu 15:17-19)."

The young man, with a hung head and drooped shoulders, humiliated and shamed, starving for food and belonging, had one option—to return home.

The father had kept watch for the son's return and, not coincidentally, he was looking down the road the day his filthy, half-dressed, shoeless son appeared on the pathway leading to the house.[101] His hopes had been realized. His son was home. Quickly he ran down the road, pulled the boy to his chest, dirt and all, and began to incessantly kiss his face. Somewhere in the midst of the father's affection, the son's practiced speech was cut short. Instead, a robe, sandals, and a ring were quickly brought and

---

[101] A. T. Robertson, *Word Pictures in the New Testament* (New York,: R. R. Smith, inc., 1930). 210.

an elaborate party was underway. Shame was erased and both family and dignity were restored.

Such a welcome for a son who has betrayed a father seems unlikely. More likely is a scene of distrust and a required trial period in which the wayward son proves the sincerity of his repentance by his obedience to house rules. Against all reasonable response, the father commands, ". . . Let's have a feast and celebrate. For this son of mine was dead and is alive again, he was lost and is found." The food was prepared—nothing but the best! The music rang out across the grounds of the mass estate. The large lawn was the perfect place for a "circle dance on the green!"[102] Servants, friends, neighbors, and families locked arms at the elbows, moved their feet to the upbeat tempo of the music, and danced for joy like there was no tomorrow!

Spoiler Alert!

Genuine, unadulterated joy on behalf of another's "found-ness" is profoundly resisted by devotion to rules and service rather than devotion to the Father's heart. As Jesus approaches his well-crafted conclusion, he cannot leave out the *other* lost son for he knows the Pharisees consider their religious compliance as the highest rank of devotion to God. The older brother, likewise, feels superior for having served his father faithfully. To celebrate a reprobate sibling was incomprehensible. The discovery of music, dancing, and feasting, in honor of such a person, flared the deep-seated resentment of having to be the *good* son—never disobeying an order, slaving to the point of physical exhaustion. In earshot of the lavish party roaring inside the house and spilling out to the yard, he notes what he perceives as the father's unfairness:

> You never gave me even a young goat so I could celebrate
> with my friends. But when *this son of yours* who has

---

[102] Ibid.

squandered your property with prostitutes comes home you kill the fattened calf for him! (Lk 15:29-30, emphasis mine.)

Saddened by the boy's lack of understanding, the father reminds his eldest that they have always been together, working side by side. Everything that was his—position and possessions—belonged to the son. He was not a slave. He had complete access to the father's attention, love, and admiration. He was family. The essentials of a ready-made-party were at his disposal . . . anytime. But now, at this moment, they "had to celebrate and be glad, because *this brother of yours* was dead and is alive again; he was lost and is found (Lk 15:32, emphasis mine)." Clearly, in the eldest son's familiarity and proximity, he never understood his father's heart of inclusion toward the sinner—the prodigal had always represented "this son of yours," never "this brother of *mine.*" The dutiful son was incapable of finding joy in his wayward brother's return to the family.

The Rebellion of Joy

Inserting ourselves into the scene of Jesus' storytelling audience, most of us would admit that we, at times, relate to the objections of the Pharisee-types. While we have not forgotten "that from which we have been saved," there still exists some level of superiority in the fact we are now "found." Judgments and prejudice regarding which lost ones are worthy of rescue keep us from the joy of a diligent search that refuses denial. Such a view deters us from mirroring the joy of a sacrificial Shepherd who goes after the one out of one-hundred. These attitudes betray the inherent value and life potential Christ places on the lost. Most certainly, we will never welcome a lost brother into the family of God if our own position in the family feels threatened or compromised. In certain instances, I still find myself questioning Jesus's reasons for eating with the "rift raft"—sinners, tax collectors . . . unclean people!

Addressing Jesus' capacity to give access and true friendship to the ceremonially unclean (some of which were also, to put it bluntly, unwashed) and promiscuous crowd, author Mark Sayers describes Jesus subversive "rebellion of joy." Getting to the root of the Pharisee's issue throughout the New Testament, Sayers notes:

> The offense of those who partied with Jesus, causing the condemnation of the Pharisees, must not be read through contemporary eyes, tainted by recent ideas of Christian stodginess. It was not the drunkenness, or possibly carousing, that truly offended the Pharisees; **it was the offense of their joy**. The idea that tax collectors, lepers, and women forced into sex work could **celebrate**. *Their lives were accursed. They were destined to suffer and lament. How dare they be filled with joy?* The offensiveness of this joy lived in a life of difficulties and limitations still exists today. Yet to many, to those filled with fear, anxiety, and despair, the joy of those who have come to the end of themselves is a light on a hill—a life lived in the Spirit, a witness to the gospel.[103] (Emphasis mine.)

Coming to the end of ourselves in order to be a witness to the gospel is where we find the greatest joy of discipleship. In a most uncensored manner, just prior to the trilogy of "party parables," Jesus had already elaborated on the cost of true discipleship. Christ declared, "Anyone who won't shoulder his own cross and follow behind me can't be my disciple (Lk 14:27 The Message)." This bold statement doesn't seem to convey much joy in following Jesus. In contrast, it seems to describe discipleship as all about *our* suffering. However, quite the opposite, our cross is not about personal suffering, though there is occasion for our formation in such; nor about our death, though there is a constant death to sin, self, and selfishness. More exactly, shouldering our cross requires an ability to *suffer with* or on behalf of another. "We never touch the realm of the Cross until we are suffering

---

[103] Mark Sayers, *Strange Days : Life in the Spirit in a Time of Upheaval* (Chicago, IL: Moody Publishers, 2017). 173.

vicariously; until suffering is the suffering of sympathy with others, and strength is being poured out in order to help others."[104]

There is never a time when we are more Christ-like than when we draw near to those suffering from spiritual or physical lack, offering help in all appropriate forms. We are not *The Savior*, but there is a sacrifice to be made on our part—a sacrifice of love exhibited in our words and actions to those the world deems as having no right to joy. This is the "stuff" Christ-followers party over!

Offensive joy manifests itself in wholehearted, count-the-cost disciples. These are Christ followers who can't think of a better party to attend or give. For the opportunity to rejoice in the "found-ness" of another, they would gladly expend time, energy, resources, and personal comforts, while never assuming they had made or *become* a sacrifice. These are believers who make disciples and teach Christ's commandments. They love God with all their heart, mind, and strength. They love their neighbor as themselves. One day his or her joy will resonate with the Good Shepherd, the tender Spirit, and the loving, grace-filled Father who saw fit to find "us" . . . never to lose us again.

An Invitation to the Party

Luke 15 serves as a conviction and an invitation. It is a conviction that has been brewing in the heart of church leaders since the tumultuous seventies. In a bygone decade of racial tension, promiscuity, and government mistrust that mirrors our present decade, God was at work. In 1974, religious leaders from 150 nations gathered for a Congress on World Evangelization in Lausanne, Switzerland. The Lausanne Covenant was created. In the introduction of the Covenant, the signing members write:

> We . . . praise God for his great salvation and rejoice in the fellowship he has given us with himself and with each other.
> We are deeply stirred by what God is doing in our day,

---

[104] Morgan, *Studies in the Four Gospels: The Gospel of Luke.* 177.

moved to penitence by our failures and challenged by the unfinished task of evangelization. We believe the Gospel is God's good news for the whole world, and we are determined by his grace to obey Christ's commission to proclaim it to all mankind and to make disciples of every nation . . . . [105]

In the realization of failure and the scope of the unfinished task, these repentant leaders boldly affirmed:

Christ sends his redeemed people into the world as the Father sent him, and that this calls for a similar deep and costly penetration of the world. We need to break out of our ecclesiastical ghettos and permeate non-Christian society . . . **World evangelization requires the whole Church to take the whole gospel to the whole world.** . . . But a church which preaches the cross must itself be marked by the cross. It becomes a stumbling block to evangelism when it betrays the gospel or lacks a living faith in God, a genuine love for people, or scrupulous honesty in all things . . . The church is the community of God's people rather than an institution, and must not be identified with any particular culture, social or political system, or human ideology.[106]

Fifteen years later, in 1989, the Congress met in the Philippines, affirming and elaborating on the highlighted statement above. Succinctly, the "Manila Manifesto" clarified the whole gospel as an integration of words and deeds: "As we proclaim the love of God we must be involved in loving service, as we preach the kingdom of God we must be committed to its demands of justice and peace." It further defined the whole church as every believer—regardless of gender, age, or nationality—called to be his

---

[105] The Lausanne Congress, "The Lausanne Covenant," http://www.lausanne.org/content/covenant/lausanne-covenant, 1974, accessed August 27, 2017.
[106] Ibid.

witnesses, for "true evangelism comes from the overflow of a heart in love with Christ." Finally, the whole world constitutes every culture, every nation, and every people group. The joy of the Church is to search for the uncommitted, unevangelized, and unreached—the lost.[107]

Between the "Party Parables" and "Cost of Discipleship" Jesus made this invitation to those wrestling with his words: "Whoever has ears to hear, let them hear." Today, we still grapple with our own discipleship and the making of disciples. We still struggle to find the best way to share our faith with others. We still harbor an under estimation of humankind and the cultures from which they come. We still view suffering as something to avoid at any cost. And, we still cling to our prejudice toward and judgment of those different from ourselves.

Post seventies, I continue to evaluate my own discipleship and witness. Post Lausanne Covenant, I want to continue to confess the timidity and fear—and, yes, my own sin that prevents the love of Christ and the proclamation of the gospel from being my constant witness. Perhaps, through his word and through listening leaders, we could once again grasp our importance to the task, the urgency to find the lost, and the tenacity to deliver Good News to those most unlike ourselves in social standing, race, gender, culture or religion. Global cities offer an environment in which to encounter God's love working among diverse people groups. "The whole church to take the whole gospel to the whole world."

Whoever has ears to hear, let them hear: *You are my disciples. You have offered all of yourself—what you have and more importantly who you are. Don't be consumed with outward conformity to institutional religion's rules or society's standards. These will make you far more judgmental than you ever thought possible. Instead, go find someone with whom you can share the good news. When you find them, love them with your words and*

---

[107] Lausanne Congress, "The Manila Manifesto," https://www.lausanne.org/content/manifesto/the-manila-manifesto, 1989, accessed August 28, 2017.

your actions, and then throw a party. The music, the dancing, and the feasting—the joy—are a witness to the gospel.

There's a party taking place this very moment. We are invited, be it as the host *or* the guest—just for the sheer joy of "found-ness!" Let's dance like there is no tomorrow.

9

Hope for The Church: Finding Center

Though every Christian Church should be a place of the widest inclusion, Christian culture has been become known as one of closed minds and closed doors.

~ Gary Comer
ReMission: Rethinking How Church Leaders Create Movement

Churches don't have the luxury of withdrawing from the community. Whether they feel wanted or not, churches must realize that the community cannot be healthy, and all that God wants it to be, without their active engagement and involvement in its life—that's the way God designed it.

~ Rick Rusaw and Eric Swanson
The Externally Focused Church

When we idealize community, we idolize community. And when we idolize church and community, we forget the one who formed it. At the very place we make the church to be the club of the pretty people, we create and imagine something that exists neither in reality nor in God's imagination.

~ A.J. Swoboda
Messy: God Likes It That Way

Walking is a passion for me. Let me rephrase that statement, walking is life to me—a sort of quasi healing for a weary body and, at times, a weary soul. If I need inspiration, need to stretch tired muscles, or relieve emotional stress, a simple brisk walk in the fresh air and sunshine (or Portland rain) makes me feel like a new woman. On one such "therapeutic" walk, during a season of physical and spiritual challenge, the usual three-mile route stretched to five. In my stubbornness, I wasn't going home until God did *something* for me, even if I didn't know what the *something* was. Close to the end of this particular *therapy session*, I crossed a familiar intersection at the far end of my own neighborhood. The two-lane thoroughfare was busy with the morning commute, so I picked up my pace and jogged across before the traffic could reach me. In my haste, I caught my shoe on a curb, and the momentum sent me flying face first into a bed of decorative rock. Stunned by the rough landing, I couldn't breathe for a minute, so I just stayed put, flat on my face as cars, trucks, and school buses whizzed by. Eventually, I regained some air in my lungs, the world came back into focus . . . and so did the bright red blood down the front of my white, hi-tech, waterproof exercise jacket.

The blood in and of itself didn't concern me. After all, there's bound to be a scratch or two where face meets gravel! Several people drove or walked past, not really looking, with one exception. A teenaged boy in route to the local high school rounded the corner, saw me and exclaimed (very loudly), "OH MY GOD!" The look of horror on his face surprised me, since all my parts were moving and I didn't *feel* seriously hurt. He kindly offered to call someone for me, but I assured him I was fine and could walk the short distance to my house.

Once home, I went to the bathroom to wash off the gravel, dirt, and blood. Then it was my turn to say, "OH MY GOD!" I didn't recognize myself. Blood covered a swollen and misshaped nose that had expanded across most of my cheeks making my eyes into slits. A broken nose looked like a definite possibility. (This fact was a bit traumatic. While I'd love to change some of my facial features, I've always been quite fond of my nose!) Removing as much of the blood as possible, I headed to the Emergency Room, looking like I'd been the victim of abuse!

A CAT scan ruled out a broken nose or an orbital fracture, as the attending physician highly suspected. The blood, in amounts that would make a prized fighter proud, was from a tiny cut on my forehead, which the doctor "glued" together. It was truly *nothing*, but it looked like *something*. What could not be seen was that a previous injury to my neck was aggravated by the fall and was serious enough to warrant weeks of physical therapy. There was truly *something*, but it looked like *nothing*.

The Church of Jesus Christ is growing in its perception of itself—learning to recognize the "nothing" for what it is, so we can give our lives to the "something" that is of God's kingdom. The Church is God's institution for the community of Christ-followers and his change agent in the world. I have every confidence this is true, and that in spite of a few misdiagnoses, the "gates of hell will not prevail."

The survival and mission of the Church notwithstanding, we are at a pivotal place in history that will require us to care far less about superficial matters (the "Oh, my God!" variety), while caring deeply about the invisible, far more serious concerns that can easily remain undetected because, simply put, *we don't see it*. In times of urban and global change, the ability to address the necessary care for the Church and the world will require a renewed focus, individually and collectively.

A Church for the Sake of Others

The Day of Pentecost (Acts 2) birthed a stunning, marvelous phenomena—the Church. God's promise to build *his* Church on the rock of Peter's confession: "You are the Christ, the Son of the Living God" (Mt 16:16-19), miraculously unfolded before a small band of one hundred and twenty disciples—the twelve (Mathias a replacement for Judas Iscariot) and several others. God's historic intention and plan was made evident in present time and place. He was creating a unique, living institution made up—of all the unimaginable things—living stones. Peter writes in a later epistle, "As you come to him, the living Stone—rejected by humans but chosen by God and precious to him—you also, like living stones, are being built into a spiritual house . . . (I Pt 3:4)."

Living stones are continually fitted together as Christ adds to his Church. They are representative of the powerful encounter and message found at the conception of the Church. The experience of the upper room— the pouring out of the promised Holy Spirit, Peter's anointed sermon, an international crowd of three thousand repenting and believing—was a home run by any evangelistic standard! Those present, literally, felt the breath of God that resembled a sudden, violent wind on a calm day. Then, the warmth of the Holy Spirit dispelled fears and doubts as "what seemed like tongues of fire separated and came to rest on each of them . . . (Acts 2:3)." All that were in the upper room were filled with the Holy Spirit and began to speak in languages they had never learned, and the multitude of guests in Jerusalem to celebrate Pentecost heard the wonders of God spoken in their native tongues. When the miracle was contested by some in the crowd as the result of drunkenness, Peter profoundly reminded the onlookers of God's promise given through the prophet Joel. This is what God had always intended: to pour, not drip or dribble, his Spirit on every kind of person, regardless of social standing, material wealth, race, age, or gender. The birthing experience of the Church emanates a timeless, powerful, and inclusive message, *"Everyone who calls on the name of the Lord will be saved."*

The hope for this kind of church growth in the Twenty-first Century remains. So much so, that because of the response to Peter's inspired preaching, we've highlighted the verbal communication of salvation to be the primary means by which the Church is built (increase in numbers and influence). However, Acts 2 offers us, his modern-day living stones, a most remarkable metric and model that is found in how the church itself was structured.

Author Soong-Chan Rah in his book, *The Next Evangelicalism: Freeing the Church from Western Cultural Captivity*, helps explain the growth of the newly birthed church more fully. He observes Luke's writing through *chiastic* structure commonly found in Greek literature. Doing so removes the imposed division between verse forty-one, "Those who accepted his message were baptized, and about three thousand were added to their number that day," and the remaining verses of chapter two. The very last verse declares, ". . . And the Lord added to their number daily those who were being saved." In *chiastic* structure, the first and last (or outside) statements are similar and focus on the central statements (verses 42-47a) which explain how the outside statements come to pass—the center is the main point. What is at the center of this particular *chiastic* structure is not Peter's sermon or the proclamation of the Word, but rather "the demonstration of the gospel in the self-sacrificial living of the church."[108] In application, Rah goes on to ask, "Have we overemphasized the personalized, verbal proclamation of the gospel while ignoring the public demonstration of the gospel—through racial reconciliation, social service, social action and justice?"[109]

Faith that permeates every aspect of our lives is a difficult teaching for, most especially, the Western church that promotes individuality. A recent pastor's blog confirmed this observation. The author made personal predictions and offered insights for the church in the coming decade. Among those projections: churches designing their buildings to be gathering spots for community, more practical pastoral ministry training, laser focused churches that know their specific mission, a wave of succession as older ministers pass the baton to younger pastors, greater funds for top-notch children's ministries, etc..[110] It wasn't so much *what* was said as the omission of critical areas of growth, such as greater urban presence—a return of the church to the city; ministry at the margins; recognition of immigrant and refugee contribution to Christian faith and church leadership; addressing justice issues on behalf of non-dominate cultures, the

---

[108] Soong-Chan Rah, *The Next Evangelicalism : Releasing the Church from Western Cultural Captivity* (Downers Grove, Ill.: IVP Books, 2009). 107.
[109] Ibid. 107.
[110] Brandon Kelly, "Future Church: 10 Predictions for the Next 10 Years," 2018, accessed Nov 3, 2018.

underserved and exploited; and the church joining the community, its public and faith-based organizations, to serve the common good.

Intentional or not, the predictions were evidence of what so many of our churches fail to see—*we* are in a self-focused rather that self-sacrificial mode of ministry. To sacrifice for a life that is lived in prayer, discipleship, a shared table, restoration of dignity to the poor, welcome of the stranger, and reconciliation—basically a life lived for the sake of others—equals a church so obviously filled with love that the Lord adds daily to our number. What exists in the middle of the modern *chiastic* story of church structure matters. Building any building from the center out is counter intuitive . . . unless it is a "spiritual house" with Christ as center.

A Place for Us

Christ's pronouncement of building his Church on the Rock was an unmistakable analogy in Hebrew culture and Hebrew Scriptures. Jesus called Peter a rock, "Petros" or a piece of the rock, but the church was to be built on The Rock, "Petra" or the essential Rock. The figurative use of the word had never been symbolic of man, but always of God.[111] His Kingdom, and the Church, consists of those who are built *into* God. The thought of being a small stone, a small piece of his Church at large, speaks to the significance and value of each individual piece. However, it also serves as a lesson in humility, never letting us forget that it isn't all about *me, my* church, *my* organization, or *my* impact on the world!

What (or *who) it* is actually about—the focus of Christ's Church—is implied in *where* Jesus chose to have this conversation with his disciples. As G. Campbell Morgan observes:

> There is certainly some significance in the place where
> Peter's confession was made, and where our Lord uttered
> His first words concerning the Church. Caesarea Philippi
> was situated at the northern extremity of Jewish territory. It

---

[111] Morgan, *Studies in the Four Gospels: The Gospel of Luke*. 211.

was a district which had been peculiarly and terribly
associated with idol worship . . . It was in this vicinity that
Herod the Great had raised a temple of white marble to
Caesar Augustus, a temple recognizing the element of
worship in the attitude of the Roman Empire to the
Emperor.[112]

Jesus, in this hostile environment of worldly culture, asked, "Who do men
say I am?" "Who do *you* say I am?" The consensus answer to his first
question: "Just another prophet." (The disciples may have omitted some of
the ugly slurs spoken about their Master!). To his second question came the
truth: "You are the Christ, the Son of the Living God." On that Rock of truth,
Jesus affirms he will build his Church.

Without too much of a stretch, I imagine Jesus was revealing where
the gospel, the truth, would be most needed and most visibly missing—in the
midst of cultural opposition. His church, the *pieces* of rock with the same
DNA and nature as the Rock, would exist for and among the culture they
were staring in the face. In *Geography of Grace: Doing Theology from
Below,* the authors bring a little more clarity:

> . . . we find Jesus in Cesarea [sic] Philippi. What is so special
> about this place, and why does Jesus choose it to ask this
> most important question of his disciples: "Who do you say
> that I am?" If you look at a map of the time, it will show
> Ceseara [sic] Phillipi to be the extreme northern border of
> Jesus' ministry—as far as we know he never ventured
> further . . . Why didn't Jesus save this riveting question for
> Jerusalem, the sacred center of an entire culture? Perhaps
> because a place like Jerusalem would have elicited a
> different answer. There, an entire history and culture would
> have weighed in, making it an unfair place for the disciples
> to consider the full possibilities regarding Jesus' identity.

---

[112] Ibid. 208.

> They needed to be removed from that context in order to
> even consider anything other than the prevailing viewpoints
> and accepted norms.[113]

Sometimes we need to engage the "world" to fully understand who Jesus is and challenge long held opinions and attitudes.

Keys, Doors, and Neighbors

When my husband and I moved to Portland to pastor an urban church, we had a significant learning curve—as I have mentioned in previous chapters. We quickly understood that the current state of this once thriving center of worship and influence, was in part due to a disconnect of the congregation from their location. They had begun to take a defensive posture *against* the "idol worshippers" out there. Change did not come quickly or easily, yet strides were made in discovering God's purpose for our place in the city.

The sign that we were making some headway came one Christmas. Like many of the churches in urban Portland, we had some architectural obstacles to overcome. The building was impressive and BIG, three acres under the roof! A section containing offices, Sunday school rooms, and the former sanctuary was built in the 1920's, but a new sanctuary had been added in the seventies. Though the intent had been to add a beautiful building to the city and neighborhood, the massive structure with its heavy, wood-carved doors had, over three decades later, become a symbol of keeping *those* people out. In other words, the urban, anti-God hostiles of *our* Ceasarea. Only nice suburban commuters (primarily white) were welcome. Of course, there were no verbal or written statements proponing such a view, nor was this the sentiment of every member. However, enough had transpired between community and church that, from the neighborhood's perspective, the attitude of an exclusive people and closed doors prevailed.

---

[113] Kris Rock and Joel VanDyke, *Geography of Grace: Doing Theology from Below* (United States: Center for Transforming Mission, 2012). 86-87.

To help remedy the "perception" the church had conveyed, on a chilly and raining pre-Christmas Day service, we propped open those intimidating doors, hired a stringed quartet to play Christmas music, provided hot cider and holiday cookies from a specialty bakery, and invited our neighbors to the festivities. Some of our "houseless" neighbors really enjoyed the treats, and a few of our "artsy" neighbors wandered in to hear the music.

Things were going well as church members mingled with new friends. That's when my husband noticed one of our long-time ushers standing in the corner of the grand foyer, arms crossed and a scowl on his face. Larry approached him to ask if he was all right. He replied, "THERE HAS NEVER BEEN ANY FOOD OR DRINK IN THIS BUILDING!" The usher had become a "protector" of a space that did not belong to him or any of us. His reversed priorities echoed the "keep them out" attitude we were trying to overcome. Larry gently put his hand on the man's shoulder and asked, "Would you close your eyes for me – just for a moment? Now, tell me what you hear." The gruffness was evident in his voice as he answered, "I hear *PEOPLE* talking and laughing." His answer sounded as if that *wasn't* a good thing but rather the unforgivable sin! With his eyes still closed, Larry said, "You know, I think the talking and laughter is worship to Jesus' ears just as much as anything else that happens in this building." The scowl softened and the following week "Joe" volunteered to head up the coffee committee—initiated as an every Sunday event in direct response to the fun we shared with our neighbors at Christmas.

Transformation is never an easy process, and especially when we are being transformed from what Soong-Chan Rah calls "cultural captivity." The church, particularly in America, has developed a culture built around rugged individualism and a "me first" attitude that is seen in our dogma and in our theology. There is nothing that challenges our often times self-centered American Christianity like the urban core of a city. We are constantly rubbing up against extreme "progressive" ideology that runs contrary to the teaching of the Bible. We have believed that combating culture with our own brand of extremism would "do the trick," but alas, we are only separated from a world to which we are called to bring the gospel—our Caesarea Philippi! How interesting it is to note that Jesus said to Peter,

> Blessed are you, Simon son of Jonah, for this was not revealed to you by flesh and blood, but by my Father in heaven. And I tell you that you are Peter, and on this rock I will build my church, and the gates of Hades will not overcome it. I will give you the keys of the kingdom of heaven; whatever you bind on earth will be bound in heaven, and whatever you loose on earth will be loosed in heaven. (Mt 16:17-19)

Jesus' disciples, then and now, needed a fresh revelation of the implications linked to Christ's kingship, but they also needed an understanding of the Church he was instituting. Jesus used the Greek word *ecclesia* to describe the Church, rather than "synagogue"—the typical word used for a place of Jewish worship. *Ecclesia* was also common in the vernacular of the day, but rather than a reference to a gathering of God's people, it was instead a reference for a "town meeting."[114] Jesus broadened the horizon of the disciples as his *ecclesia* or called out ones—called out to do Kingdom business—with keys, not to lock out or exclude, but to aggressively pursue righteousness and shalom. The Message translation rephrases Christ's response to Peter's confession beautifully,

> . . . God bless you, Simon, son of Jonah! You didn't get that answer out of books or from teachers. My Father in heaven, God himself, let you in on this secret of who I really am. And now I'm going to tell you who you are, *really* are. You are Peter, a rock. This is the rock on which I will put together my church, a church so expansive with energy that not even the gates of hell will be able to keep it out. And that's not all. You will have complete and free access to God's kingdom,

---

[114] Morgan, *Studies in the Four Gospels: The Gospel of Luke.* 212.

keys to open any and every door: no more barriers between heaven and earth, earth and heaven. A yes on earth is yes in heaven. A no on earth is no in heaven. (Mt. 16:17-19 The Message)

Jesus still desires to tell us, his Church, who we really are. We are not huddling behind massive doors—ones that often grace our exquisite buildings—in order to keep the world out; but opening those doors, figuratively and literally, to our communities.

Grace and Vulnerability

Open doors offer freedom. They press the Church to enter and exit for the sake of others, allowing God's grace to penetrate places and hearts—including ours. Too often, we have suppressed our need for grace and therefore our giving of it. Whether we recognize it or not, solidarity with the suffering of others can only lead us to grapple with our own vulnerability and the grace we need to survive. "Solidarity makes us human. It bears witness to how out of control suffering makes us all feel."[115]

The uneasiness that accompanies our experience of suffering, personal or that of others, can often be linked to an imbalanced representation of the "celebration and suffering"[116] seen throughout Scripture and in our present culture. Recently, a friend missed a phone appointment and texted me that he was having "first-world" problems. Being the "with it" *older* woman I am, I did not want to ask, "What the heck are you talking about?" Instead, I quickly consulted Google. Urban Dictionary—a highly reputable source (I jest!)—defines the term as "Problems from living in a wealthy, industrialized nation that third-worlders would probably roll their eyes at," *or* "when you already have a substantial amount of what you need, [but] complain about the quality and type you

---

[115] Ron Ruthruff, *Closer to the Edge: Walking with Jesus for the World's Sake* (Birmingham, Alabama: New Hope Publishers, 2015). loc 417.
[116] Rah.The Next Evangelicalism,143.

want.[117] Superficial "issues" such as an internet connection going down for fifteen minutes, or deciding which of my ten jackets to wear today, or the fact my seven dollar latte was made with only one shot of espresso instead of two, or the gift of a new Toyota instead of a Mercedes. Could it be that too much blessing has led to such privilege that we have formed a misconception of what it means to actually suffer? Has such belief, in turn, led to a necessary denial of any kind of pain—unless that pain is associated with a trite first-world problem?

During a particularly difficult season of ministry life, I remember writing to a friend, "The pain is so deep, the ache so unrelenting. I have tried to pray it out, cast it out . . . and throw it up, but no relief is in sight!" Her response, after a chuckle at my dramatic terminology, was to keep coming to the Cross. "You are doing the right thing, turning to God and not away from him." I followed her advice. Regardless of how unfounded my feelings, I shared them with Jesus. Three years later, in yet one more prayer for God to heal my hurt, a gentle voice spoke: "You have felt marginalized. I know what that is like. Use the pain as a reminder that, in small measure, you have felt the same anguish as those economically, socially, or ethnically marginalized . . . it is as close as you will ever come to understanding *their* pain . . . and *mine.*"

Suffering can be a gift that moves us to self-sacrifice. It helps us understand that the Resurrection (celebration) and the Cross (suffering) are two inseparable realities of our faith and of the community known as the Church. "The intersection of the two threads provide the opportunity to engage in the fullness of the gospel message."[118] Theology "arising out of the context of abundance, but unfamiliar with a theology arising out of poverty, suffering and marginalization" can prompt us to minister to the poor from our privilege and power rather than "genuine mutuality and reciprocity."[119]

---

[117] Urban Dictionary, "First World Problems," Urban Dictionary, accessed November 6, 2018.

[118] Rah.155

[119] Ibid. 155

Our experience of suffering, and God's grace in the midst, can help us open the door, walk across the proverbial street, encounter those who suffer greatly and find even greater depths of God's grace among those he loves.

The book, *Geography of Grace*, tests two assumptions: 1) "Grace is like water—it flows downhill and pools up in the lowest places" and 2) "If we are going to test the limits of grace, we must be willing to be wrong."[120] In the first assumption, the authors challenge that:

> If we want to experience deeper levels of God's grace, shouldn't we take a swim in the places where God's grace pools up? Do the people and places most marginalized and ostracized by the mainstream society and the church actually hold a prophetic vision *for* us all?[121]

In the second assumption they state,

> Our proclamation of the gospel is often a product of the power and privileges we enjoy. Therefore, if we are to teach and preach good news to the poor who live at the mercy of the dominant culture, and who endure the theological categories we produce, we must be willing to take great risks. The gospel of Jesus' liberating word invites us not only to examine, but also to challenge and even subvert, if necessary, "orthodoxy" as it is defined and practiced by the mainstream church. In other words, we are invited to reclaim the Bible's liberating Word for the world and risk being wrong about unexamined assumptions and long-held beliefs that in reality do great harm in the name of being 'right.'[122]

So much of what has brought the Western church to a stalemate of ineffectiveness has been that which we fail to challenge in ourselves: superiority, individualism, materialism, prejudice, self-centeredness, etc.

---

[120] VanDyke.
[121] Ibid. 18.
[122] Ibid. 19.

Vulnerability, on the other hand, opens our hearts and our lives to find true grace, to help and be helped. Then, and only then, will we stop screaming, "Oh my God," at the insignificant nothings of life and recognize the somethings we thought were nothing. We will become the self-sacrificing church of Acts 2 that multiplied because of who they were at the core: Little "Rocks" ready to risk everything to make sure the *nothing that was something* was set right. This is the hope. May we once again find our center as the Church of Jesus Christ.

Part 3

Surrender

The following pages contain stories of urban practitioners whom I am privileged to know as friends and colleagues—fellow Christ-followers who have fearlessly obeyed God in the face of great personal risk. They have discovered their own desperate need for God in the places that so desperately need him. In the discovery of God himself, risk has given way to the blessedness of total surrender. May the collective narrative of their journeys inspire us all.

10

Risky Dreams: Street Surrender

[We look, as children, in desperate dependence to our heavenly Father. This is not a resignation of [our] gifts or passions or training, but a deployment of those endowments to a place beyond safety, beyond [our] ability to control the outcome and beyond [our] power to succeed. It's a place where God is desperately needed and a work in which he delights to engage—for it is his own work.

~ Gary Haugen

Just Courage

You're blessed when you are at the end of your rope. With less of you there is more of God and his rule.

~ Matthew 5:3

The Message Bible

Security is mostly a superstition. It does not exist in nature, nor do the children of men as a whole experience it. Avoiding danger is no safer in the long run than outright exposure. Life is either a daring adventure or nothing.

~ Helen Keller

In a small, inconspicuous office—just large enough to hold a desk and two chairs—our church-led Food Pantry conducted a brief check-in for regular and new guests. On more than one occasion, it was my joy to welcome an incredible array of humanity into a space where they could shop the four food groups, conveniently designated by color, and leave with a healthy balance of free groceries.

"In-take," as we called it, was a favorite volunteer duty. It allowed me to individually connect with every person entering the pantry, learning a little about his or her background and circumstances. The Oregon Food Bank required pantry workers to ask for an address, income level, and the number of people living in a single household. The questions often prompted guests to give brief context for their answers. The "facts" requested and offered didn't tell anyone's complete story, but often gave insight to how long someone had been on the street, if they were staying with a relative or friend, or if an illness or hardship had caused them to lose the ability to earn a living. Some would share hopes of a job possibility or new living conditions.

Beyond stated information, there was the obvious—deep lung-hacking coughs from living outdoors; glazed eyes from the lack of sleep, drugs, or alcohol; hands caked with street grime; etc. Regardless of any individual's present state, they were welcomed with a genuine smile—and often a handshake. I hoped the friendly gestures would let each person know they mattered, but I must admit, the bottle of hand sanitizer under the desk was my best friend! *A squirt or two of the alcohol infused gel will keep the clients safe from 'germ-share,'* I reasoned. But truth be known, my concern was for myself and the possibility of contracting some mystery disease. (My dream of being the next Mother Teresa is highly unlikely!)

The admission of mild mysophobia tendencies on my part is an awkward revelation of the minimal risks I've encountered to extend God's love in tangible, human terms. I've learned that the risks we take to serve others, big or small, must be understood in the context of Christ's surrender to the will and purpose of the Father. Jesus did not flippantly gamble on our salvation by putting his life at risk. Rather, he and the Father, immersed and overcome with love, willingly died for us, confident that those being loved would have opportunity to so love. *We never surrender to risk itself; we surrender to Love.* Therefore, when Christ-followers risk their own well-being, comfort, reputation, security, or safety on behalf of others, they are confidently and willingly yielding their lives to Love Himself. Love draws and sustains us. Love is what prompts us to dream risky dreams . . . kingdom dreams.

Wrong Place, Wrong Time, Right Dream

Kingdom dreaming is a risky venture that often defies common sense, expediency, and the rationale of security or success. Just ask Simon Peter . . . or James . . . or John. These fishermen had their dreams transformed after a long night of fishing and zero "catching!" The sea had refused to yield its bounty, and Peter (Simon) and his friends called it quits for the day. Peter pulled his boat to shore and began washing the nets, when Jesus jumped in and asked him to "put out a little from shore." *OK, I was thinking of heading home for a nap, but he is the Teacher. There are many people trying to hear. I get it. Sure, I can do this simple thing.*

The water serving as his megaphone, Jesus taught the crowd from Peter's boat. When he had finished teaching, he asked Peter to go further out into deeper water and let down his nets for a catch. (G. Campbell Morgan jokes, "He finished teaching, and now, positively, he is going into the fishing business with them! "[123]) Teaching was Jesus area of expertise, but fishing was Peter's. There was no way they were catching anything. The place and the timing were wrong—Peter, James, and John had just fished here . . . all night. Nonetheless, this experienced fisherman responded, ". . . because you say so, I will let down the nets." The catch that day was enormous—so great,

---

[123] Morgan, *Studies in the Four Gospels: The Gospel of Luke.* 73.

the nets began to break and they had to call in their partners from BestCatch.com to help with the fishy harvest (Lk 5:1-11)!

As the fishing business took a turn for the better, Jesus called Peter, James, and John to leave their nets and follow him. And they did. Peter and his friends risked following a man that was about to teach them to dream differently. They were about to "catch" men and women instead of fish. This new dream required a different outlook . . a new perspective . . . a deeper trust. Simon Peter was used to lowering his net in the right place at the right time to catch the right fish. He, with his companions, were used to sorting the catch, throwing out the "suckers" in favor of the "keepers." Jesus, on the other hand, didn't seem to follow tried and true trowler's rules when fishing for fish *or* for disciples. When it made no human sense to do so, he offered unconditional love; his net of invitation was woven in a "whosoever will" pattern; and his intent was to keep every flailing "fish" he pulled out of the drink.

Peter's lessons in this revolutionary new kind of fishing would be many. He would need the Master's direction and assistance, but he *would* leave everything and follow a dream—not of a Galilean fishing empire successfully getting fish from the sea to markets on land, but of (most literally) transferring humanity from one kingdom to another. Today, Jesus asks us to surrender to the will and purpose of the Father by surrendering to His love. He asks us to fish for men and women in a pool of humanity found in unfavorable conditions, at a time and place that challenges our own reasoning. He invites us to share *his* dream.

City Dreams

Joining this alternative, Christ-infused, God-informed, kingdom-minded dream are those who live and work closest to the "fish." Allow me, at this point, to offer a disclaimer regarding the "fish" metaphor: we are not out to lure people in only to eat them for dinner! Christ's words hold no hint of usury or personal gain. When we fish for men and women, our only "bait" is the offer of a transformed life that embodies the holistic work of God. But in order to make that offer, we have to go to where the hungry fish are. The streets of our major cities are literally full of *hungry people.*

The last statistical information available from the U.S. Census Bureau reveals that, in 2017, almost forty million Americans were living at or below the poverty level.[124] While poverty rates, including the nation's child poverty rate, have fallen since the 2008 recession, it's important to note that specific racial and ethnic groups still experience poverty at a rate that exceeds the national average.[125] Poverty is the root cause of a myriad of social issues faced in urban centers—including food insecurity and homelessness or the inability to sustain a residence—common results of diminished income. According to the National Alliance to End Homelessness, over a half million people were experiencing homelessness on a single night in 2018—a number derived from HUD's Annual Point-in-Time Count. Of the half million counted, sixty-seven percent were individuals and thirty-three percent families with children. Among individual persons, youth under the age of twenty-five and veterans respectively represent seven percent; eighteen percent represent those who are "chronically homeless" and consist of people with disabilities or those who have been homeless for an extended period of time.[126] The data is alarming and leaves us with more questions than answers.

Digging deep into the issue—causes and solutions—is the focus of Dream Centers dotted across some of America's major cities. Matthew Barnett, pastor of Angeles Temple Foursquare Church and co-founder of the L.A. Dream Center, has effectively mobilized the church to address poverty, abuse, and addiction with free services and resources. Since its inception in

---

[124] U.S. Census Bureau, "2017 Poverty Statistics," 2017, accessed April 15, 2019, https://www.census.gov/search-results.html?q=percentage+of+US+citizens+living+under+the+poverty+level&page=1&stateGeo=none&searchtype=web&cssp=SERP&_charset_=UTF-8.

[125] Annie E. Casey Foundtion Foundation Kids Count Data Center, "Children in Poverty by Race and Ethnicity," https://datacenter.kidscount.org/data/tables/44-children-in-poverty-by-race-and-ethnicity#detailed/1/any/false/, 2018, accessed April 25, 2019.

[126] National Alliance to End Homelessness, "Homelessness in America," accessed April 25, 2019, https://endhomelessness.org/homelessness-in-america/homelessness-statistics/state-of-homelessness-report/.

1994, denominational leaders and pastors have utilized the Dream Center model to reach the most vulnerable in their communities. These leaders have done the unthinkable . . . followed Jesus on an unreasonable, high-risk (maybe even reckless) fishing expedition!

City Dreamers

Meet Sheila

Sheila Donegan is a five-foot, petite built woman with a determined, no-nonsense demeanor. The current director of the Boston Dream Center recalls the day Jesus asked her to "leave her nets" and do what many would consider foolhardy and irresponsible. The Boston native had lived in California for thirty years, when in 2012 she heard God say, "I want you to move back to Boston. Sell everything. Take nothing for the journey."

Sheila immediately began to prepare . . . but, in reality, preparation had begun years prior. Born in a city that Governor John Winthrop of the original Massachusetts Bay Colony hoped would be a shining example of the biblical city on a hill,[127] Sheila's childhood was engulfed in darkness. Her father was an alcoholic who committed suicide when she was just five years old. When she was sixteen, Sheila and her mother moved to the west coast hoping for a fresh start in a new place. However, in her early teens, Sheila followed her father's path of addiction. As an under-aged offender, she was in and out of Juvenile Hall. As an adult, she was arrested for drunk and disorderly conduct twice in a two-week period. She vividly recalls the officer at the precinct desk looking at her and saying, "I know you. You were just here two weeks ago." Sheila did not want to be *known* at the jail. The profound shame she experienced led her on a five-year journey to sobriety . . . and the no-conditions love of God she discovered through Christ.

In the years that followed, Sheila served her church organization and spent some time as a missionary, but this new call came at a greater

---

[127] Wikipedia, "Nicknames of Boston," https://en.wikipedia.org/wiki/Nicknames_of_Boston., accessed April 27, 2019.

cost. She would be leaving her home with nothing and going to nothing—no job, no place to live and no idea of what "the mission" was . . . yet! To make matters more *interesting*, Sheila felt directed by God to NOT raise any funds. In a real sense, she was leaving all her "nets." More than a surrender of possessions, it was, quite literally, a surrender of her entire life.[128]

Meet Brad and Stella

Two hundred or so miles north, the New York City Dream Center had been underway for three years prior to Sheila's move to Boston. Brad and Stella Reed had been an intricate part of the L.A. Dream Center. Stella had served for thirteen years in worship and youth ministry leadership, and Brad served as the boy's home director and later an associate pastor for just slightly less years than Stella did. The couple met and married while at the center and felt they would be there for a lifetime. From very different backgrounds, each had their own unique point of surrender.

Stella grew up in a pastor's home with a positive experience of church and a growing relationship with Christ. After high school, she was university-bound, but before freshman year began, Stella wanted to "check out" the Dream Center. The community's need, and the valuable resources being leveraged to alleviate that need, immediately captured her heart. The center had just purchased the old Queen of Angels Hospital and the ministry on the streets was growing fast. Stella never made it to her college destination. Instead, she would receive a degree in compassion, mercy, and incarnational ministry as she lived among and loved the people of inner city L.A.

Brad, like Stella, was raised in church but didn't choose to follow Christ until he was, in his words, "dramatically saved" as a young adult in Alabama. Shortly after making a commitment to Christ and while seeking direction for next steps, he heard a voice say, "Look up the Dream Center." Without questioning the vivid inner prompting, he typed the words into his browser. (Brad tells this story in a matter-of-fact fashion as if to confirm that

---

[128] Sheila Donegan, interview by author, October 10, 2018

everyone knows God leads and guides us with a Google search!)
Immediately after finding an address and obtaining basic information, he
boarded a Greyhound bus bound for Los Angeles. Brad still chuckles over
what happened next: He was expecting to enroll in an internship program,
but soon discovered he would be placed in a discipleship school . . . for
addicts! Oh well! No one seemed to pay any attention to the fact that neither
in the past or present did he have a substance addiction. Brad stayed with
the men in the recovery program for years, eventually becoming a volunteer
leader and later a staff member.

After their 2004 marriage, Brad and Stella became licensed
ministers, happily serving the Angelus Temple family and the L.A. Dream
Center for another 5 years. In 2009, the center began sending teams to New
York City. The Reeds were aware that the work was going to require people
and pastors on location. They suspicioned, at some point, they might be
asked to assume a role. Content with their present assignments, Brad and
Stella were in the midst of remodeling a long awaited for home. Moving their
young family across the country wasn't the practical or sensible next step. As
illogical as it seemed, Brad and Stella could not dismiss the idea. After much
prayer, the Reeds came to believe that they would indeed be asked to lead
the efforts in NYC. When the request came, their answer would be, "YES!"
That single, surrendered "yes," once uttered aloud, took them from the
largest west coast city to the Borough of Harlem and the largest city in the
U.S.[129]

Meet Craig

On the other side of the nation, shalom is at work in a city whose
name means peace. Salem, Oregon's capitol, is located in the serene and
beautiful Willamette Valley. The city is home to yet another Dream Center
co-founded by Director Craig Oviatt over 15 years ago. Craig's involvement
in city outreach began as a result of "hitting bottom." A successful
businessperson and church member, Craig found himself facing a horrific

---

[129] Brad Reed, Stella Reed, interview by author, August 10, 2018

divorce that presented him with a six-figure debt. The fact that he held an executive position with executive pay wasn't enough to cover spousal support and pay the bills for two households. Craig moved into his office to survive. He lived on seventy-five dollars a month, and for the first time in his life, he knew what it meant to truly experience hunger. At one point, he joined Bella, his pet Beagle, for a bowl of dog food—and enjoyed it.

Left with almost nothing, Craig entered a season of drawing close to God. The Bible became his safe place. He began to journal his observations, keeping a detailed record of the ways Scripture applied to his life. One rare sunny Oregon Saturday, Craig retreated to the parking lot of his office to read and pray. The reading plan for the day included the Old and New Testament passages of Job 29 and Matthew 25. Craig recalls, "I now understand why Satan couldn't turn Job [a blameless and upright man] from God. After having everything taken away, what Job cherished most was the man he was *for* God. If I survived, I wanted to be like Job." Turning to the New Testament passage about the separation of the sheep and the goats, Craig says, "Wow, this is the last moment on earth and Jesus was saying that, what was most important to him, is how you treat people. How you help people. How you extend his love . . . his arms. Then I realized Job *lived* that." Craig wrote in his journal, "If you [Lord] give me an opportunity to do this, I *will* do this." He signed and dated his journal entry. Recounting that moment of commitment, Craig humorously acknowledged, "Apparently, that's a contract!"

The next day, a Sunday, Craig got his opportunity. Pastor Todd Gould, a staff pastor at West Salem Foursquare Church, preached a sermon that touched on both Job 29 and Matthew 25 as a basis for his vision to begin a Dream Center—a ministry that would serve the under-served of the Edgewater neighborhood in Salem. God had Craig's undivided attention. At the close of service, the pastor asked for those interested to come forward for more information. Craig almost dove over the chairs to get to the front.

Later, during an interview at the church, Craig was asked how he'd like to participate. He ran quickly through a list of repair and service jobs he could do, and closed with, "I'll scoop dog poop out of people's backyards, I just want to be there." Ryan, the interviewer, replied, "No . . . I want you to be a block pastor." Wondering what part of dog poop-scooping Ryan didn't understand, Craig argued that he was *not* a pastor. "I can't quote scripture. I've never led anyone to God. I don't know anything about theology." Ryan interrupted, "And that is why I want you to be a block pastor." He assured Craig that he possessed the necessary "pastoral" qualifications—the humility and willingness to serve neighborhood need while caring for neighbors and volunteers with the love of Christ. In God's not-so-subtle way, he reminded Craig of the *"if-I-have-an-opportunity-contract."* At that point, there was no arguing. Craig simply responded, "I'm in!"[130]

On the Other Side of Risky Dreams

Surrender to God's love ultimately produces a love for people and places. Sheila, Brad and Stella, and Craig would experience an overwhelming desire to see their cities transformed. For each, that kingdom-focused dream is now realized daily in Edgewater, Harlem, or the Boston Common—and it was worth the risk.

Boston Common

The risk for Sheila came not only in the form of leaving every material possession behind, but also her preconceived ideas of what ministry in Boston would look like. She felt God had clearly asked her to plant a church in the heart of the city, but was *uncomfortable* with the traditional church planting models. For almost two years after her arrival in Boston, she wrestled with whether or not she was actually supposed to pastor a "church." The struggle for the *what* gave way to a multi-faceted dream for the city. In prayer, God spoke to her heart, "Forget everything you know about church. If you didn't know anything about what 'church' looked like, what would you imagine the church to be?" Sheila felt free, for the first time in years, as she realized that church doesn't have to be four worship songs and a three-point

---

[130] Craig Oviatt, interview with author, September 14, 2018

message in the confines of a building. She pictured a church in motion—on mission—in the streets. Church, for Sheila, looked more like an AA (Alcoholics Anonymous) meeting—people contending together for freedom through storytelling and accountability—with the purpose of living differently in the real world, the world outside of the meetings they attended. Theologically, it agreed with the New Testament idea of the church as "called out ones" (*ecclesia*). A church structured around mission and community outreach made sense!

What also made sense to Sheila was the formation of a Dream Center, of which she unabashedly declares "*is* a church." She began Boston Dream Center with an outreach to the Suffolk County Jail. Coming full circle from the shame of her own arrests, Sheila offered Christ's forgiveness to every "prisoner." Her message of unconditional love so resonated with staff and inmates, she became known as "The Forgiveness Lady." The nickname became God's reminder to Sheila that she was indeed *known* at a jail, but this time for an entirely different reason. Instead of reaping the consequences of her own addiction—the indignity and humiliation of multiple arrests—Sheila now had the honor of dispensing grace and restoring dignity in a place where the two were in short supply.[131]

East Harlem

Brad and Stella felt prepared. They had done the "urban thing" well and for over a decade. They were experienced practitioners. However, upon their arrival in New York, the Reeds realized that what *worked* in LA would not work in NYC culture. For one thing, the Big Apple—a moniker used in a 1970's tourism ad campaign—was a walking, not driving city. The anger of LA drivers was contained inside a car; here Brad and Stella experienced the frustrations of New Yorkers up close and personal on the street.

The Reed's also noticed that gentrification in their new city often meant that Section 8 Housing existed directly across the street from multi-million-dollar homes, highlighting the city's economic disparity.

---

[131] Sheila Donegan, interview with author, Oct 10, 2018.

Furthermore, the high cost-of-living caused a regular ebb and flow in residency that made relationships with neighbors difficult or, at the least, temporary. In addition, LA, home to the mega church, was not typical in NYC. Buildings or meeting places were not easy to come by . . . or cheap.

All of the above factors meant that, even for experienced "city folks," the risk of failure in New York was great. Brad and Stella instinctively knew they would need to let the city shape them or it would break them. Their surrender to God was irrefutable . . . now it was time to surrender to the streets of Harlem. God would shape and forge a new way forward in the east while maintaining the same dream of city transformation.[132]

Edgewater

Craig's journey took him from desperation to dedication, from a "contract" with God to the streets—the very location from which Salem Dream Center was launched. Every Saturday, in a parking lot just on the other side of the Willamette River in the Edgewater neighborhood, volunteers and block pastors would gather, organize, and then go door-to-door to meet their neighbors. One home at a time, the city became a series of faith-building steps for Craig.

Craig recalls when he began to understand faith as an essential element for ministry on the street. One Saturday morning, early in the Dream Center's mission, team members gathered in the designated location ready to go door-to-door. Just before they dispersed, a car pulled up and the driver asked Craig, "Are you the Dream Center? Are you the church people who help neighbors?" "Well . . . yes," Craig replied with curiosity, "Can I help you?" The man briefly explained that as his young family prepared for a day at the Oregon Coast, "My wife *insisted* we pray first." After the prayer, she emphatically instructed him, "Go get a box of diapers and a box of formula, we need to stop on our way to the beach and drop off both items to *those church people*. Someone needs them." Craig accepted their gift with gratitude and then attempted to hand the boxes over to Todd, the outreach

---

[132] Brad Reed, Stella Reed, interview with author, August 10, 2018.

leader, who refused, saying, "They gave them to you, so you are the one who should give them away."

The need for diapers and formula was unlikely. Craig's assigned area within the Edgewater neighborhood was primarily made up of older residents. In previous weeks, he had not encountered babies at any of the twenty homes he visited. He tried again to push the baby products toward Todd, but Todd simply repeated, "God had the couple give them to you . . . so, you take them!" Realizing he wasn't going to win the argument; Craig walked to his car and placed the items in the trunk rather than needlessly carry them through his section of the neighborhood.

Craig didn't know it at the time, but God was about to solidify his reliance on the Holy Spirit to connect needs and resources. At the nineteenth home, a woman named Linda in her late fifties, came to the door. Craig introduced himself and ask her a few routine questions, the last of which included, "Can I pray for you?" The woman responded, "I'd like you to pray for my granddaughter. She is here with me today because her husband beat her up." The granddaughter appeared in the doorway with a significant black eye and a baby in her arms. Soon the grandmother disclosed that her granddaughter had no formula or diapers for the baby and no money to purchase either. With a gleam in his eye, Craig said, "I had a couple give me diapers and formula. I'll go get them from my car." The young mother asked, "Are they size four diapers?" Then she added, "The formula needs to be Enfamil AR. Is that what you have?" Craig replied, "I have no idea, but hold on, I'll be right back." He ran the five blocks to his car, retrieved the "drive-by gifts," and returned to the home with, you guessed it, size four diapers and Enfamil AR formula in hand. Craig became acutely aware he was not in this alone. The all-knowing God of compassion saw the need—be it diapers for a mom or increased faith for Craig—and moved on the hearts of both the givers and recipients![133]

---

[133] Craig Oviatt, interview with author, September 14, 2018.

Craig's capacity to believe and trust God was enlarged beyond measure. Linda came to faith in Christ soon after learning the story behind the diaper and formula miracle. Her granddaughter, Jasmine, followed suit a few weeks later. Jasmine's husband, once a gang member, eventually chose to follow Christ. To this day, he is a hard-working, loving husband and father . . . who often volunteers at the Dream Center!

Dreams Come True

The ministries of the Dream Centers mentioned above have a combined service history of thirty years. Their stories, in biblical fashion, do not focus on perfect leaders, perfect cities, or perfect programs. They do, however, reveal the unfolding of God-sized dreams in the midst of blessing and struggle.

Boston Dream Center

In the five, almost six years of their existence, Boston Dream Center operated out of Sheila's small apartment, later a basement office, and finally a larger facility located on the Boston Common. The organization's goal of reaching the chronically homeless, impoverished, addicted, and incarcerated with immediate services has been realized through a number of partnerships and programs. Joining with the Boston Food Bank, BDC fed over five thousand people in the first year of their existence. Later, a mobile food truck was added to supply fresh produce, and other necessary food and hygiene items, to the Charlestown Housing Project and disabled seniors located in the Watertown neighborhood. Working with the Department of Transitional Assistance in Boston, BDC provides CarePacks (bagged groceries and necessities) for homeless and low-income families that lack the documentation to receive state food assistance. Monthly outreach to those living on the street provides food, clothing, and connection in the community. In cooperation with the Suffolk County Jail, BDC hosts health and wellness, spiritual care, and life skill classes. During the first four years, hundreds of men participated, and post-incarceration life coaching and care are currently in motion.[134]

The multi-faceted ministry Sheila had envisioned came to pass in spite of the common non-profit fund-raising and location dilemmas. Following BDC's five-year anniversary celebration, the board, staff, and team members gathered to assess and realign their efforts. After a close review and concerted prayer, they realized that the prison ministry, known as BDC Inside/Out Jail Ministry, had seen the greatest transformation of lives to date, reaching over eight hundred men with three hundred commitments to Christ. It made sense to focus their people, resources, and mission toward those directly affected by incarceration. At the same time, Sheila was presented with an opportunity to expand the scope of the prison ministry in Southern California at the LA County Jail. In a remarkable and bold step, the BDC Inside/Out Jail ministry is in the process of becoming a bi-coastal effort.

Sheila's heart resonates with a deep love for the most marginalized. She knows how many incarcerated men (and women) have been forgotten. BDC saw the need for a holistic solution that included housing and employment. With a seventy to eighty-five percent recidivism rate, it was obvious that a comprehensive support system is essential—during incarceration and upon release. The Inside/Out Jail Ministry plans to meet this need for Suffolk County and LA County through the creation of discipleship groups for men and women inside their respective facilities, intentional aftercare and discipleship for each person upon release, live-in discipleship homes, ministry to incarcerated youth, and care for the families of the incarcerated.

The plan is clear and the team is determined. Sheila is confident God will supply the strength and resources. Her move to Boston was a step of surrender. The risky dream was well worth the results and Sheila concurs

---

[134] Boston Voyager, "Meet Sheila Donegan of Boston Dream Center Downtown Boston," http://bostonvoyager.com/interview/meet-sheila-donegan-boston-dream-center-downtown-boston-heart-city/. 2018, accessed September 12, 2018.

with Winnie Mandela, "There is no stopping an idea whose time has come." I would add, ". . . especially when it is God's idea!"

Dream Center NYC

The Reed family have been in New York for more than a decade. The innovation, creativity, and "can-do" attitude that shape the narrative of the city has also shaped their approach to urban ministry. Brad notes that, "Without resilience, a self-identity based in who you are not what you do, and a dedication to longevity, the city can eat you up!" The latter of these, longevity, is rare not only for ministers but also for New Yorkers in the business, education, medical, or entertainment sectors. Permanence, while an uncommon characteristic, is the very attribute by which Brad and Stella established a Dream Center and a church. A constant and dedicated presence in the city has enlarged their view of the gospel to encompass evangelism integrated with mercy and justice.

The embrace of a wider and deeper gospel opened their eyes to God's work in places others might not notice. For instance, they saw a city that has led the way in the development of programs for the disabled, created inclusive public education, and devised efficient ways to service their citizens—from mass transit to garbage removal. These are points of grace for all who choose to call NYC home.[135]

Finding grace already at work, the Reeds saw the Dream Center as a means to bring connectivity between city services and religious non-profits. They have partnered with the NYCHA (NYC Housing Authority) whose mission is to connect low and middle-income New Yorkers with safe and affordable housing. They are active participants at local community board meetings and partner with local food banks. At the same time, they regularly connect with other city ministries actively working for the common good. The Reeds make it their business to know what other churches and non-profits are doing, so needed services are not replicated and/or a

---

[135] Brad Reed, Stella Reed, interview with author, August 10, 2018.

collaboration can be formed. Current lists of services, public and non-profit, are kept updated and ready as a referral guide.

In this spirit of collaboration, the Dream Center NYC states its mission as "Partner[ing] with local communities through programs designed around identity, empowerment, purpose, and community engagement in order to see neighborhoods flourish across New York City."[136] Currently, the Dream Center has a number of initiatives that have made an impact, particularly in the East Harlem and Chelsea neighborhoods. The Adopt-a-Block Program helps underserved families who reside in public housing by meeting practical and relational needs. Community markets offer access to healthy foods and block parties create a fun, life-giving atmosphere for neighbors to connect. Neighborhood dinner parties are hosted for residents to encourage authentic community over food and laughter.

The need for practical help and relational connection is also extended to those faced with housing insecurity and those experiencing isolation. DCNYC created the Restore Program as a holistic outreach to those experiencing homelessness. Temporary relief—food, personal hygiene items, blankets—is offered, but referrals to a number of city services, including housing options, give these New Yorkers an opportunity to renew their dreams. The center's "Visits" program is the result of a collaboration with local social workers providing DCNYC with the ability to successfully connect trained volunteers and vulnerable neighbors, such as the disabled, elderly, and sick—anyone living in the community but isolated from it.

As one might imagine, all of these programs engage people as whole beings and serve physical, emotional, relational, and spiritual needs. To help holistically serve the city's needs and promote the sustainability of ministry, the Dream Center hosts Short-term City Mission teams and a ten-month Leadership Program for young adults. The teams and students engage with the Dream Center Programs and with the Dream Center Church's ministries.

---

[136] Dream Center NYC, http://www.dreamcenter.nyc., accessed March 20, 2020.

In this way, the Reeds are incorporating a clear integration of city mission and the church's engagement with the *whole* city—one borough and one neighborhood at a time.[137]

Hope for all NYC's neighborhoods has recently extended the Dream Center's ministry to the working-class Brooklyn neighborhood of Bushwick. In a unique partnership, Metro World Child, a faith-based humanitarian organization committed to serving underprivileged inner-city children around the world, has invited the Dream Center to help with their local efforts. In doing so, President Bill Wilson of MWC offered the use of their Brooklyn facility for DCNYC's staff meetings, intern/training programs, and as a second campus for the Dream Center Church. Their team is busy helping develop unused portions of the former hospital. (Old hospitals seem to resonate with Dream Centers across the country!) After a decade of faithfulness to their city, they see God's commitment to the people of NYC— not through their efforts alone, but because of the partnerships, support, creativity, and the generosity of others.[138]

Brad and Stella acknowledge other NYC pastors and ministries as a primary reason for their continued presence in the city. They have developed a sincere appreciation for the non-competitive relationships formed with other NYC Christian leaders. There is a real sense, especially as church planters and service-oriented ministries, that they need one another for encouragement *if* they are going to go the distance in the city.

Going the distance with them is Pastor Tim Keller of Redeemer Presbyterian. Tim has had substantial influence in the Reeds lives, just as he has influenced so many NYC pastors and urban church planters around the globe. Redeemer's programs, Hope for New York and City Ministry Year have created the means for church leaders to learn and work together. In a recent training session attended by Brad, Keller mentioned the two reasons, why city ministry is so hard: (1) There are so many people *not like you,* and

---

137 Ibid.
138 Dream Center NYC, onsite interview, December 13-15, 2019.

(2) *there are so many people like you . . . but better!* His comments were prompted by the diversity of race, culture, religion, socio-economic standing, etc., and the intense excellence of talent, intellect, and creativity large cities naturally draw. He accompanied his remarks with this realistic exhortation: "You either dig down to a place you didn't know existed or you leave." The Reeds have dug down to the very source—Jesus and his love for the poor, the marginalized, the city—and they have STAYED. Risking failure truly was a surrender to His love.[139]

Salem Dream Center

What began as a church outreach blossomed into a self-sustaining, fully functioning Dream Center in Salem. Craig, a dedicated member of the team, progressed from a volunteer block pastor to a paid staff member tasked with the center's development. By his side, Pastor Todd Gould spearheaded the creation of a free medical clinic, staffed by the volunteer hours of local physicians and nurses. Eventually, the clinic became its own non-profit, and Craig was named director of SDC.

The ensuing decade and a half has seen the center grow in influence and community service. Craig has been an astute student of his city, and in particular, the Edgewater District. On their current website, SDC notes:

> On October 2, 2004 a group of people stepped out in faith
> and took a walk on the Edge [a reference to "Edgewater"],
> moving into a community of poverty, hunger, gangs,
> violence and darkness. We walked into the Edgewater
> District with a commitment to love people exactly as they
> were, without expectation or condition. To build
> relationships that transitioned into lifelong friendships. Our
> desire was to help people realize their value, to break the
> fangs of a starvation mentality, and to help people transition
> out of poverty into lives of sufficiency. We have stayed true
> to our commitment, and become a positive part of the

---

[139] Brad Reed, Stella Reed, interview with author, August 10, 2018.

Edgewater District. We stepped to the edge, and we pushed back darkness.[140]

Craig recalls that as the center was creating new programs for a myriad of city concerns, a friend and fellow non-profit director challenged him to narrow SDC's efforts. Craig and his volunteers had obviously reached a breaking point of what they could accomplish in addressing the needs of the homeless, released prisoners, gangs, kids and families in the neighborhood. "Choose one," his friend dared. When Craig could not, he bluntly announced, "I'll choose for you." He paused for affect, and then continued, "What is the one area you just thought, *he better not forget . . .?*" Craig's quick yet determined response was, "Families. I choose children and families." Since that time, family units have been at the heart of every SDC program. As they focus on education, mentorship, and food sufficiency for children, parents are served in the process. This is where Craig's passion has always been, it simply took another perspective to define, refine, and then ensure God's dream for Edgewater.

A family-focused SDC has watched a neighborhood begin to dream again. Over the course of the last fifteen plus years, Salem has seen a consistent drop in the Edgewater crime rate, with a thirty-two percent lower occurrence of juvenile crime compared to communities with similar demographics. Vandalism has dropped by seventy-nine percent. The middle school, in the heart of "the Edge," went from having one of the lowest academic achievement standards to one of the highest. The graduation rate has increased from sixty-three percent to ninety-eight percent, with one-hundred percent of teens active in the center's program graduating.[141] The key to SDC's success could be summed up in one word: relationship. Craig notes, "Charity happens when strangers are altruistic. Transformation happens when you help someone in the context of friendship."

[140] Salem Dream Center, "A Walk on the Edge," http://salemdreamcenter.org., accessed March 20, 2020.
[141] Center

Building friendships happens every Saturday with neighborhood children attending an open gym at a local school. Volunteers go beyond just the creation of games; they listen to children and help them navigate through the many secondary effects of poverty. Breakfast and lunch are served to make sure the kids get a nutritious meal on the weekend. Field trips and outings, including those to high schools and colleges in the area, help kids envision a successful future. In the last year (2019-20), the center developed Nuestra Casa (Our House), a learning center for children and adults offering tutoring, computer stations, English language classes, and practical life skills such as sewing, cooking, and nutrition. Nuestra Casa is, literally, a "house" and the back yard serves as a community garden. In addition, SDC provides services at apartment complexes—home cleaning and repair assistance, arts and crafts for kids, etc.—and several holiday outreaches that provide food and gifts for Christmas and Thanksgiving. All of the centers programs begin with making friends.

SDC has experienced profound success, but as with the Boston Dream Center and Dream Center NYC, they are grateful for and dependent on partnerships in all sectors. Several West Salem churches help sponsor projects and provide volunteers. Close to fifty corporate sponsors, representing businesses ranging from a local auto dealer to a global athletic chain, have joined with SDC to make a difference. Craig has been intentional about connecting with local city and government officials—many of whom, including police officers, find time to volunteer at SDC.

The center's flourishing volunteerism is due, in part, to a unique strategy. SDC has no time requirements for their volunteers. If they find they can't show up for a given event or program, someone is always there to fill the gap. As unlikely as it may seem, there are always more than enough helpers. Craig states, "Once they show up, they are hooked." (Every non-profit could use a few more volunteer "addicts!") Certainly, there are seasons when a volunteer will need to step away, but Craig has been amazed by the long-term faithfulness of so many and by God's faithfulness to have the right people present and ready to serve.[142] SDC has become a place where the served and the servants learn to dream again.

Three Dreams Among Many

Just as the Lord called Peter, James, and John to follow a risky new dream that would result in transformed lives, so Sheila, Craig, and the Reeds have followed Jesus to the risk-filled streets of Boston, New York, and Salem. They have defied common sense, good timing, and sometimes their own capabilities to "put out a little (or a lot!) from shore" and catch a glimpse of the dream Jesus had in mind for a specific city, community, or neighborhood.

A mere sampling of Dream Centers dotted across the U.S., these are three examples among many non-profits in my church organization that have participated in a network that has led the way for others to dream big in their communities. They have, together and individually, opened the hearts of pastors and leaders to the kingdom potential of underserved places and people.

Points of Wisdom

From Sheila

Sheila says, "When you give [surrender] it all, God restores it all. The restoration is not just for those you serve and befriend, *it is for you*. Sheila's restoration was not material, but something far greater: personal transformation that comes from sharing His grace and love in the very place she experienced the greatest pain.

From Brad and Stella

Brad shares the story of him and his young daughter running into a homeless man on the streets of NYC. Because they were on their way to an

---

142 Craig Oviatt, Compassion Network Presentation, October 2018.

appointment, they walked past the man and then turned back. Brad pointed their "street friend" to the Dream Center's food outreach, knowing he was hungry. His little daughter looked up, finally grasping with her young heart their family's purpose: *"Daddy, that's what we do isn't it? We help people."*

From Craig

Craig despises charity. Sounds odd considering his role in the community. But over the years of being imbedded in the Edgewater neighborhood, he has learned that giving a coat to someone who is cold may warm their body, but may also tear away the last fiber of their self-respect. However, if you get to know the person and choose a coat for them, it warms their body and their heart. *There is a fine line between enabling and supporting—relationship helps dissolve the line.*

11

Risky Business: Incarnational Surrender

Incarnational ministry is very much like osmosis. Osmosis is when two cells touch each other and the molecules of one pass through the cell membranes into the other cell. In the same way, incarnational leaders expect to see change for the better in both themselves and the community.

~ T. Aaron Smith
Thriving in the City: A Guide for Sustaining Incarnational Ministry Among the Urban Poor

Over time . . . many [church] planters began primarily harvesting the most visible and easily discernable fruit (people that would enter a church meeting place), without taking the time to invest in abundant seed sowing (going outside of the building to evangelize). Aggressive seed sowing was sometimes ignored because it did not produce quick results.

~ Linda Bergquist
City Shaped Churches: Planting Churches in the Global Era

. . . Jesus' incarnation is our model of love for the other. In the same way, when he calls us to take up our crosses and follow him, he does not intend for us to believe that our deaths will redeem humankind, but he does intend

that our lives would be lived in imitation of his self-sacrifice.

~ T. Aaron Smith
*Thriving in the City: A Guide for Sustaining
Incarnational Ministry Among the Urban Poor*

*They will rebuild the ancient ruins and restore the places long devastated;
they will renew the ruined cities.*

Isaiah 61:4

The twenty-year period in which my husband and I served in various levels of denominational leadership was irrevocably marked by our time in the city of Portland. The role of urban pastors gave way to the role of overseeing a district of churches with a focus to renew the connection between church and community. God must have known we needed a challenge, fresh convictions, and above all, a flexibility that would allow us to sponsor a creative reach into cities.

The personal changes we experienced were forged in the cutting-edge ideas and foresight of leaders attempting new ministry models that would reach urban neighborhoods—whether in Portland or cities across the U.S. These were models with the potential to develop and revitalize every facet of community life. One of our favorite proposed "models" was a young leader who boldly approached my husband with his idea for a non-profit pub and a church operating side by side. Larry asked Pastor Ryan a few probing questions and discovered a heart-felt, God-directed intent to provide a public gathering space for neighbors while directing profits to organizations, local and otherwise, that work for the common good. The idea would allow neighbors to enjoy a great menu, build relationships, and rub shoulders with an incarnational church. In addition, the concept allowed for participation with non-profits looking for sustainable solutions to civic issues, youth and family support, economic development, and environmental concerns to name a few. The approval for such a venture was considered "controversial" in some church circles and, jokingly, earned us the moniker of the "Pub District" for quite some time.

Like Ryan, many have realized that reaching the urban core of cities requires more than the one, two, three of suburban church planting. The spiritual and economic need in such areas also necessitates the cooperation of business, city government, neighbors, and church functioning for community benefit. At times, the bringing together of these entities happens when the church initiates and operates a small business. At times, entrepreneurial ministry and business become one-in-the-same to activate city transformation. Finally, at times, the collaboration is large-scale community development organized in cooperation with a multitude of churches, businesses, non-profits, and city services.

Into the Deep

Luke 5:1-11, as mentioned in the previous chapter, is the story of three men willing to take a risk and follow Jesus. This is not just a fishing story; it is also a story of *mission*. When Jesus asked Peter, James, and John to head out to deep waters and let down the net, subsequently filling that net to the brim, he illustrated the enormity of the need (the bounty of fish) and a mission that would be completely beyond their capacity (the limitation of the net). The following are stories of urban missionaries who have seen the magnitude of need in city centers, realized their limited capacity, and risked going into the "deep" waters of urban ministry anyway! These Christ-followers and leaders have learned that to know your community is to live among them, listen to them, and become "one of them"— just as God became human and joined us.

City Immersion: The Thomas Story

Jason and Susan Thomas were staff members at a thriving rural church in Illinois. Native to the Midwest, steeped in an all-American way of life, the couple was poised to assume a lead pastoral role following the rapidly approaching retirement of the current pastor. They were comfortable and content in every material way. Their three boys were happy. They loved the church and the community in which they served, but something was stirring in their hearts—a longing for something more. Rather than mere churchmanship, they wanted to see their commitment to Christ lived outside church walls and traditional venues of Christian service. The emotions they experienced were inexplicable, but the God-led direction was sure.

The way forward inadvertently became clear when the couple met with my husband and me at a denominational conference. Having lived in the Portland area for about five years, we had fallen in love with the city. Our conversation rotated around the good things that were happening in Rose City neighborhoods and among the churches we served. Jason and Susan were intrigued because they had always heard Portland described as a "dark" or spiritually hard place. For our young friends, the view of God-movement in a liberal, independent, post-Christian city served either as a revelation of the Spirit or the ramblings of a couple of eternal optimists! Regardless of the source, the Thomases were inspired enough to visit Portland, return to Illinois to sell their home and most of their belongings, and move to the city just eight short weeks after our initial conversation.

Susan and Jason immersed themselves in Portland culture. They rented a small apartment in Northwest Portland near the historic Alphabet District. A local Starbucks hired Susan as a barista and Jason went to work for Northwest Family Services, a public non-profit that supports family stability for at-risk children. *Doing* life in close proximity to their neighbors lent itself to growing relationships. In getting to know people, they were often struck with what they refer to as "an openness to question . . . everything, including God." Coming from an area of the country that would generally accept faith and church as a part of life, here many had abandoned their faith traditions. At the same time, Portlanders were uncharacteristically open to faith conversations.

The ingenuousness was refreshing, and Jason and Susan quickly grew to appreciate the honest dialogue and sincere friendships they were forming. In an effort to create a space for continued conversation, the

Thomases believed a coffee shop would help them further connect with the community. Building on Susan's quick rise from barista to manager at Starbucks and Jason's long-time hobby of roasting coffee beans, the two pursued ownership of the oldest, independent coffee shop in the city—Coffee Time.

Church Time is Coffee Time

The risk of a coffee business in a city with, almost literally, a coffee shop on every corner (sometimes two!) was substantial. However, Coffee Time was not just a business to the Thomases; it was an opportunity to build relational credibility. The intention was not to leverage business in order to do ministry, but to do business with the mission of serving people. The quality of coffee would be critical in this caffeine-saturated town, but more vital to their success would be personal availability to newfound friends— this would be their "business." As unorthodox as it may have seemed at the time, Jason and Susan were learning a fresh perspective on what it means to pastor outside a formal church setting.

In the years to come, the Thomases would expand their business endeavors. A second location was opened, they began roasting and marketing their own beans, and Jason created a cold-brew coffee that is now distributed by local and national retailers. Business growth led to Susan's appointment as the president of the local business association, giving both her and Jason an opportunity to affect systemic change. They helped improve city policies for small business owners, brought awareness to business owners' impact on the environment, and promoted business collaboration during times of internal and external challenge. While broader issues of their community are of concern, the one-on-one personal ministry—especially among staff and customers—remains the hallmark of their life in Portland.

Living, working, conversing, listening, recreating, and standing with neighbors is evidence that the Thomases have incarnationally embedded in their community. With a history of traditional ministry positions, Jason and

Susan have found that the lack of a formal pastoral role has, ironically, released them to lead much like any church pastor. Susan says, "When people discover we *are* pastors, they simply reply, 'That makes sense.'" Their constant presence naturally leads to friendships among the marginalized, church-adverse, and those dealing with physical, emotional, and relational issues. The pastoral oversight offered is never contrived, ever bound by grace, and *spontaneously intentional.* The Thomases readily admit that a decade ago they would have said, "We love our neighbors. We love our community. We love people far from God." But that version of their Christianity—the version that often confused religious overwork for kingdom activity—had no idea how to connect with people who held differing philosophies or worldviews. Now they daily interact with those who struggle to assimilate in the traditional church "box." They see through the eyes of others and love them until they find a way forward to faith.

Seeing is Knowing

Conversion in this ministry model is a long walk of obedience. It is building Christ's Church one person at a time. It begins with a geographic location—a city neighborhood—and the people that share that "place." Church planting in this model is painstakingly slow. The years spent, thus far, have helped Jason and Susan envision a church in which the "members" first encounter Christ through steadily built relationships; those developed on the street or over conversation in one of their coffee shops. Susan laughs as she describes the eclectic clientele. "I walked through Coffee Time one morning to find a church group having Bible Study in the back room, a practicing Wiccan in the main seating area, and a guy in a window seat dressed like an elf peering into a crystal ball." These are the people, along with the intellectuals, agnostics, homeless, wealthy, gay, straight, homeless, artists, drug addicts, young, old, sophisticated, and humble that make up their Northwest neighborhood. Jason and Susan consider every one of them worthy of God's love, and so they love and disciple—yes, pastor them. Conversion and the formation of a church are not a goal to be reached, but both have been and will be the result of creating space in the community for relationship to blossom.[143]

The idea of putting friendship first is not new in church planting, but it is not always the first choice. Author Linda Bergquist acknowledges two methods of church planting. The more common approach has a new church as its goal and requires a strategic business model of investors and profitability. The less common approach is when the goal is to meet a specific need and a church or network of churches result from that ministry—often among the poor or marginalized. Of both she asks some poignant questions:

> Nevertheless, what if ministry, evangelism, discipleship and church planting are initiated not simply to meet needs, but to acknowledge every individual as worthy of love, respect, appreciation, honor, and access to the gospel? Such an approach means that no person can stay invisible. Good business, maybe not. Real goodness? Yes.[144]

For the Thomases, coffee is good business, but ministry or church planting is not about investors, funding, or profitability. The *real goodness* is that no person encountered is overlooked—no person invisible. Jason and Susan appreciate the dominant church planting model, but the people who frequent their shops and stroll the streets where they live need Jesus to intersect their world with his grace, love, and mercy. They need a ready access to the gospel that does not require them to conform to anything but the Person of Jesus, represented without compromise by many believers in Northwest Portland, but most certainly by Jason and Susan Thomas.

Creative City Reach: The Bono Story

Sal Bono was raised in a Catholic-Italian-Immigrant home in Detroit, Michigan. While "Christian" in the sense that he regularly attended

---

[143] Jason and Susan Thomas, interview with author, August 12, 2018.
[144] Linda Bergquist and Michael D. Crane, *City Shaped Churches, Planting Churches in a Global Era* (Skyforest, CA: Urban Loft, 2018).107

mass as a child, Sal had never made a commitment to follow Christ. He did, however, have a deep desire to know God and read the Bible from cover to cover . . . more than once. What disturbed Sal regarding Christians and church was the lack of evidence that they were "living out the pages" he had diligently read. That God existed was a strong conviction, but equally as strong was the certainty that he wanted nothing to do with church.

Sal's opinions changed quickly when he met Krystal at a Detroit bar where he worked as a bartender and she was a server. Krystal had a vibrant relationship with Christ, and so did her friends. Together, they quickly took on the task of praying for Sal. These "friends" chose not to judge Sal or his lifestyle. They simply loved him. When the invitation came to go to church, he went. Sal recalls, "I gave my life to Christ not because the pastor gave a great message or because the music was so outstanding, but because of this group of friends who lived the pages."

Sal and Krystal were married not long after his newfound faith. They shared a background in the arts—Krystal was a vocalist and Sal had worked as an actor in Los Angeles—and the desire to minister to young people. Their calling and gifts made way for them to work with Generation Acts, a Florida-based worship arts program for college students. They traveled the country and performed with the students for close to six years. The Bonos then moved to the West Coast where Sal had accepted a position with Apple in San Francisco. In addition to his new tech position, he and Krystal also served on a church staff.

Going Home

The Bono family was enjoying California life and Sal was loving the team approach integrated by Apple. Home, church, and work could not have been better . . . until Sal came across an article about his home city of Detroit. The piece described a new non-profit organization helping the city out of decades of social and economic decline. "The Empowerment Plan,"[145]

---

[145] Empowerment Plan, https://www.empowermentplan.org/about) 2020, accessed May 1, 2020.

a workforce development program, began with the simple idea of a college student: make coats for the homeless that convert to sleeping bags. The founder and current CEO, Veronica Scott, soon realized that while the homeless needed coats/sleeping bags, they needed jobs. She put those living on the street or in shelters to work and, to date, every hire represents an employed, housed, and productive resident of the city.

The story touched Sal deeply. A usually unemotional type, he wept uncontrollably. He cried over the devastation and need present in his hometown and felt irresistibly drawn to return. He and Krystal took a couple days to pray. They knew what they were supposed to do, but thought it would likely take several months to settle things at work and make arrangements for a cross-country move. Two days after their confirmation in prayer, Sal's boss, knowing nothing of his *pull* back to Detroit, informed Sal that Apple in Troy, MI (a Detroit suburb) was looking for someone with his skill set and start-up experience. Just five short weeks later, Sal, Crystal, and their family were back in Detroit.

The Detroit they found in 2012 was far different that the Detroit of Sal's childhood. Though still largely African American, the city had grown more diverse. (Sal jokingly remembers that, as a child, he saw an Asian man out for a jog. It was so unusual, his first thought was, "Who's chasing that guy?") The welcomed diversity was tempered by the city's rapid gentrification. Large corporations and financial institutions acquired deserted properties cheap. Though both diversity and gentrification have their positive effects—creating cultural depth and jobs—poverty remained a primary issue in Detroit. Economic displacement was prevalent. Rents were increased to force residents out, allow landlords to make a tidy profit, and big business or property managers to buy at under market prices. Individuals and families who had been long-time, sometimes generational, residents of downtown Detroit were forced to leave their families, friends and way of life. Thankfully, after the first wave of displacement, the mayor stepped up and intervened with rent control, returning a measure of stability.

What does Detroit Need?

This "new" Detroit required an adjustment. Sal and Krystal originally thought they would find a building, hang a "shingle," and have church. But after taking time to walk the streets of their neighborhood, meet and talk to neighbors, they changed their minds. The people they engaged with were not opposed to Christ, but church had left a negative impression. In fact, the three churches located a block from the Bono home had near-empty parking lots on Sunday mornings. Worse yet, downtown Detroit was home to a handful of multi-million-dollar church buildings located in some of the most economically devasted areas, sending the message, "We don't care about the community." Sal and Krystal began to ask if yet another church building was needed? Was there another way? How could they effectively share the love of Jesus? Never opposed to starting a church the traditional way, they understood that simply announcing, "Here we are!" wasn't going to work.

What would work was based on the make-up of their community. Employment at Apple in Troy allowed Sal and Krystal the time needed to get to know their immediate neighbors. They discovered a lot of small, middle-class business owners trying to make a go of it in a city slowly reviving. Younger entrepreneurs filled the classrooms of Wayne State University and the College for Creative Studies—both institutions located in their "backyard." The latter focused on majors in advertising and communication design, photography, entertainment arts—including digital film and animation—giving the neighborhood a resonant ingenuity and resourcefulness. Equally represented were residents living well under the poverty line and the homeless. Sal and Krystal knew they had to reach all of these distinct groups to bring community transformation.

Inspired by the Empowerment Plan, Sal began with the immediate need, but had a more sustainable solution in mind. He and Krystal enlisted a few new friends to help distribute meals in the park. The caveat was that no one could simply give a "hand out," they had to eat with the recipient. This allowed all members of their community time to interact and build relationships. The soon-established friendships encouraged other community activities, including partnerships with local schools to provide school supplies and clothing. On a lighter note, Sal arranged to live-stream the Michigan/Michigan State football game for the entire neighborhood—an event most neighbors could never afford to attend. As meaningful as each activity was, the next steps would restore jobs to the most vulnerable of their Detroit neighborhood, enrich the lives of neighbors regardless of their socioeconomic standing, and work wholeheartedly for the common good in Detroit.

A New City Label

Sal's goal was to open a space for start-ups and small businesses to incubate—develop and mutually learn from one another. Students would work with owners as free-lance employees or apprentices to help get businesses up and running. Once successfully launched, businesses would hire from the community to help neighbors rise out of poverty. To work towards this goal, Sal created *Branded by Detroit* which upcycled materials from the countless abandoned homes in downtown neighborhoods. From salvaged wood, the newly formed company created signs, furniture, and even photo transfers. The popularity of the products grew exponentially when displayed at the oldest open-air market, Eastern Market, in the city. Sal recalls the difficulty he had convincing the directors of the market to allow participation of *Branded by Detroit* as a vendor. The newly formed company overcame reticence by showing up at the market to paste two thousand sticky notes bearing the *Branded by Detroit* web address. It caught the director's attention! When he looked at the website, he was so impressed, he gave the go-ahead for the company to sell their wares. The director also observed that the sticky-notes littered the entire site requiring hours of clean up. He warned Sal, *"Never do that again!"*

Branded by Detroit was a starting point and provided a number of local jobs. Sal also began a digital marketing company and studio that employed local college students. Both companies did well, but the marketing company grew exponentially and their clientele extended beyond Detroit to large corporations around the country. The success drew the attention of a program sponsored by Goldman Sachs, known as 10,000 Small Businesses. Sal was asked to participate in six months of classes which prepared him and the digital business to grow in profitability. Then, Sal, Krystal, and their team began to notice their community connection decreasing. They stepped back to take a long look at what they were doing and why they had come to Detroit. Their calling was urban and the mission was local—they were urban missionaries. Doing business as mission meant their decisions were not based on what was best for the business, but rather what was best for the mission.

Mutually, they came to the conclusion that *best* for God's mission meant a return to their work with local startups that would, in turn, connect *all* the people groups of their neighborhood. Sal closed the national digital marketing business and began to focus on *Branded by Detroit*. They rented an old warehouse and hired a friend to help transform the building into an affordable co-working space. They used the new shared space to bring together entrepreneurs focused on story-telling technologies, such as podcasting, website design, video production, and local digital marketing. Gradually, they morphed back to the original goal of community relationships, business development, and neighborhood renewal formed along the local socio-economic spectrum.

The return to mission sparked a new idea. The Bonos and their team had discovered a multitude of incredible life stories among long-time Detroit residents. Sal was convinced that these stories needed to be heard. Utilizing the co-working space, neighbors, business leaders, civic leaders, students, university personnel, the homeless – whoever wanted to come—received an open invitation to hear a guest Detroit resident share their story. "Detroit Stories," an official event title, brought meaningful connection, community collaboration, and an appropriate sense of city pride.

The Unseen Harvest

Sal and Krystal, like so many Detroit residents, developed a newfound respect, if not outright awe, of God's restorative work. Their seven years in Detroit proved to be fruitful, and as Sal notes, "There is a harvest we will never see." Combining the worlds of ministry and creative business, though often misunderstood, allowed the couple to help others begin viable and sustainable businesses with a vision for community focus. They saw neighbors come to Christ and facilitated a number of small group Bible studies for discipleship. They collaborated with other non-profits, and Sal taught marketing and entrepreneurship classes designed specifically for non-profit organizations. Sal was often a guest panel member for Detroit Startup, Inc., and gained influence throughout the city.

The visible fruitfulness, however, paled in comparison to the impact God had on their hearts. The constant call to stay with the "mission" often challenged what made sense and took a toll on personal finances. However, looking back, Sal recognizes that his missiology was reinforced with the urgent need for creativity in "urban-out-of-the-box" ministry. At the same time, he gained new admiration for traditional church models and a partnership that says, "We need a healthy mixture of all this going on to see what God has called [the church] to become." The need for a *community of faith* is greater than ever. Sal and Krystal, rather than defend the validity of urban mission (and missionaries!), have come to value the greater Mission— one accomplished in a multitude of ways and through a multitude of people and organizations.

The mission for Detroit can be summed up in one of Sal and Krystal's favorite memories. Shortly after their arrival in the city, they held an outreach event to help feed the homeless. Serving as volunteers that day were two college-aged, white, upper middle-class non-Christians. On their way to feed the homeless, they happened across a man that had been stabbed in the park. He was bleeding, so they took him to a local hospital and waited for him to be treated. On his release, they found a local CVS

Pharmacy and purchased the man new glasses—his "readers" had been broken in the park altercation. Later they learned that, Cedric, a victim in the moment, was a convicted felon who had just been released from prison for aggravated assault. After a trip to the hospital and pharmacy . . . and knowing what they now knew about the man they were helping, the volunteers could have considered their job done. Instead, they pursued a friendship that has kept them in touch with Cedric over the years. Cedric's life, along with the lives of two "green" volunteers, has been forever changed as a result of the kindness shown and relationship established.[146]

That day, Sal and Krystal saw a rare and unlikely breakdown of class, socio-economic, race, *and* faith barriers in their Detroit neighborhood. This was the initial "picture" of what God had placed in their hearts—people caring for people because they have humanity in common. The renewal of a place and the restoration of a people continues in a city primed to creatively reach its neighbors with the genuine love of Christ and transformational good. A new harvest is on its way!

Sunrise for Community Development: The Ketch Story

Long-time volunteers with the local church and foreign mission's development, Brad and Lynn Ketch looked forward to the day when they could devote themselves full-time to city issues. A primary concern was the number of people living in extreme, generational poverty—a group they advocated for often. Brad served as the Chairman of the Board for a non-profit homeless shelter, bringing his business and economic expertise to the table. Lynn, raised by parents working in the public health sector, grew up in Native American and low-income areas of the U.S. She followed her parent's footsteps as a public healthcare professional.

Brad and Lynn had seen firsthand the lasting devastation of those living far below the poverty line. They made the mid-life decision to step into "full-time ministry" just before the 2008 financial crisis. The years they had

---

[146] Sal Bono, interview with author, October 30, 2018.

spent in the business and healthcare sectors was the financial and experiential platforms from which they would pursue mission. However, the recession created a complete reversal of their personal finances. Having never based a major life-decision on the availability of money, the Ketches resigned from their positions, and joined ministry "*with* the poor." Brad confesses, "Instead of entering into service *to* the poor from a point of strength and financial security, we entered at a point of identification. I don't think God would have had it any other way!"

The newfound solidarity with the poor and the professional acumen possessed by both Brad and Lynn, played significant roles in their future service. Lynn, from her health systems background, had been trained to look for the social determinants to health and the environmental factors that contribute to poor health outcomes in a community. Brad's economic and financial background prompted him to explore the reasons for the inability of so many in the U.S. to rise from poverty to prosperity. The Ketches recognized that relief efforts, though essential, were not enough. Systemic factors of poverty (and its related issues) had to be addressed. The undeniable missing piece in conquering generational poverty was development.

The Ketches felt their greatest contribution would be realized in community development. The next step, they assumed, would play out locally. Instead, Brad was recruited by a major, international non-profit as the CEO for their operations among the ultra-poor of the Philippines. The position was a temporary, one-year commitment, but Brad and Lynn felt inclined to accept. While there, they were privileged to watch relief and development work together to provide jobs and sustainable income to the poorest of the poor. The community development principles practiced in the Philippines were "repatriated" along with Brad and Lynn on their return to the U.S.

Forming a Community Development Corporation

Home for the Ketches is Gresham, Oregon where Brad was born and raised. Their residence is located just blocks from the Rockwood Neighborhood, the poorest and most diverse neighborhood in Portland. It is here that Brad and Lynn listened to a community of immigrants, displaced African Americans, and Latinos to discover, not what they could do for the neighborhood, but what the neighbors, given the right tools, could do for themselves. The Ketches realized that with development as a goal, they would face obstacles of welfare mentality, systems and political hierarchies rooted in race, and civic power structures. They knew there would be some resistance from fellow Christian non-profits and churches steeped in relief programs or events. Notwithstanding complications, they began conversations with neighbors, city and state government, and area churches to collaborate in the formation of a community development corporation.

The inclusive conversations resulted in a true understanding of the community's assets. Residents were invited to participate in small, language specific and culturally sensitive groups, known as "Rockwood Speaks," to discover one another's neighborhood experience and ascertain available resources. The information from those gatherings was brought to a larger event, known as "Rockwood Listens," to determine collective action. Rockwood Listens included church and civic leaders, but their primary function was to listen. Table facilitators were chosen from the community and representative of many of the over eighty-eight ethnic groups in the neighborhood. From these initial meetings, Rockwood Community Development Corporation (RCDC) was formed.

Sunrise Center Opens

RCDC, as described at the close of chapter five, currently operates Sunrise Community Center. The once functioning restaurant had closed, and the potential buyer was planning to open a strip club. The city intervened, purchasing the building and, in turn, offering it to Brad. The redeemed location, with its commercial kitchen, made way for a number of new businesses run by community members. In 2019, the center was home to twenty-two ethnic food makers/caterers and several community start-ups that utilize eight available cubicles. The large event space is often used for weddings or parties, in addition to three local churches that hold church services in the facility. The kitchen, workspace, and event room are rented at below market rates and help sustain RCDC programs held at the center and throughout the community—including legal clinics, an English institute, job training, business incubators, an adult day care for local Slavic refugee seniors, and the Shalom Network of local churches who live, pray, and work for the benefit of Rockwood.

The programs of the RCDC gave way to larger community ventures that are transforming housing infrastructure and food security—two of Rockwood residents' greatest concerns. Brad formed Oregon Community Capital, Inc. to work with investors and foundations in order to secure the EDA's (U.S. Economic Development Administration) Opportunity Zone[147] financing for private investment in distressed communities. Rockwood will benefit from an upcoming project that includes hundreds of units of affordable housing. The new housing, to be located in close proximity to the Sunrise Center, is targeted for those who earn below eighty percent of the area's median income. RCDC is helping its partners take the program statewide through Opportunity Zone Conferences, of which five were held this year. While Brad drives community investment strategies, Lynn has created the Food Systems Collaborative to help the fifty percent of Rockwood residents who grocery shop at gas station marts. Non-profits, government agencies, for-profit food businesses, and even community gardens are working to bridge the gap in food production, processing, distribution, and consumption for a community that flourishes.[148]

---

[147] U.S. Economic Developement Administration, "U.S. Economic Development Prioritizes Applications for Projects Located in Opportunity Zones," https://www.eda.gov/news/press-releases/2019/06/12/opportunity-zones.htm 2019, accessed May 12, 2020.

[148] Community Development Corporation of Oregon, "2019 Annual Report," https://www.rockwoodcdc.org/wp-content/uploads/2020/02/CDCO-2019-Annual-Report.pdf), 2020, accessed May 13, 2020.

Alarmed by the Gospel

Rockwood is beginning to see the signs of a thriving community. The successes celebrated above have not come easy. Brad, Lynn, and their team have faced the misunderstanding of once supportive civic and church leaders. They have had their reputation questioned even as they have been lauded for the work God is doing. They have faced personal and organizational financial challenges right along with the generosity of community members and corporate sponsors. Brad describes the work of community development as "hot" and, most unfortunately, it is often *too hot* for those who are risk adverse. Following Christ costs everything, and "gospel demands are not just challenging or uncomfortable, they are alarming. If you aren't alarmed by the gospel, your understanding is not the gospel."

Brad and Lynn are constantly alarmed by the gospel—alarmed at how close God is to the poor. They are alarmed at how *poor was* their experience of God, and his heart of justice, until they came face-to-face with profound poverty . . . for a long time. They, like other Christians working in the field of community development, construct a framework around justice that drives biblical outcomes. Brad admits that it's easy to get "prophetic, frustrated, or even angry" when others aren't as aware of injustice and/or the need for biblical justice. Brad consistently reminds himself and others that "justice is not a framework, concept, or formula . . . it is a Person. The personhood of Jesus enfolds the [entirety] of justice. [Christ's] view of what needs to occur is the only next thing." Brad and Lynn endeavor to walk alongside Jesus, following his lead—even when, at times, he doesn't follow the rules! They understand that justice, wrapped in Jesus, will be patient with others as they journey toward a richer knowledge of His love and mercy.

The journey towards Jesus-justice is not a mere fad. Listening to the voice of the Lord, and listening to the community itself, is an ever-evolving process. Brad jokes about the way in which many of his young, white, upper-middle-class volunteers throw around the popular expression *"woke,"* and its counterpart phrase *"stay woke"* with abandon. These hopeful social justice warriors often morph the meaningful term that originated decades ago among African Americans. The phrase has more recently been revived to bring awareness to current racial injustices. The convolution for these young, exuberant activists is found in an incongruity between awareness and action. The tendency to assess *who* has been awakened to injustice is common, but it is often accompanied by the unfortunate side effect of judging *how* "woke" others seem in comparison to the "ideal." Brad, smiling, quotes a Captain Kirk line from Star Trek Beyond: "We're not doing what we should do, but what we can do." Justice, in very un-faddish ways, is seen in community *develop-ment-ing*. It is a gradual movement toward the kingdom on earth as it is in heaven. Or in Brad's words, "I like my way of doing it, better than your way of *not* doing it!" Community development is a long-haul operation, but we can be confident that "nothing [God] wants in a community will be denied."

A Resilient Wall

The continual move toward just and whole communities is not just about fixing systems or institutions—including the Church. It is about the transformation of perspective—especially as it pertains to biblical justice—that begins with a changed heart. "We think if we fix all the systems, people will be fixed, but that isn't true." Respectfully bringing together the systems that embody policies and politics (city, county, federal government and government agencies) with the faith community holds the hope of *change* in all of us. Brad sees RCDC as the hub or backbone that helps bring a multitude of area systems together. He is convinced that the rise of non-profit institutions, like CDC's, across the country are "filling a third space" that link and hold communities, cities, and regions together. There is caution to not overestimate *or* underestimate the power systems hold, but to understand that the kingdom of God is ever-present as his people engage and work with others to correct policies and change hearts.

Brad and Lynn are elbow deep in community development—and it is messy. They often console themselves with Nehemiah's rebuilding of the walls of Jerusalem, a *beyond* messy undertaking! Nehemiah went about reconstruction with untrained help using burned and broken pieces of the once glorious city. Brad observes that when archaeologists uncovered the wall Nehemiah rebuilt, "They knew it was *the wall* . . . because it was a *really crappy wall*. It's a wall no one would ever build (with those materials) if you had a choice. *But* it's been standing for three thousand years." Brad and Lynn understand that the challenging job of joining a hurting community right where they are, using the assets at hand—whether broken people, broken systems, or broken materials—will create resilient, flourishing systems and cities for the coming generations. While the hope for a bright future is sure, each day the sun rises, God's kingdom is more clearly seen and more fully realized in Rockwood.[149]

Going Deeper

The fishermen/disciples (Peter, James, and John) witnessed Jesus fill their much-too-small nets, so when the invitation came to go with him into the "deep" of their current day cities and villages, it was less about the size of the nets and more about what he could do—anything! It was less about their methods and more about how *he* chose to incarnationally reach the world—sometimes one-on-one, sometimes in crowds, sometimes through provision, sometimes through healing, etc. This was the mission his disciples were invited to join.

"God's mission has a Church," is a common phrase used by missiologists and theologians to describe the primacy of God in the missional equation—it is *his* mission on *his t*erms. The expression also helps define a singular, though multi-faceted, mission: We are invited to join God in his present pursuit to redeem and reconcile all things. As the church learns to look beyond concepts or models of traditional ministry, God's

---

[149] Brad Ketch, Interview with the author, September 7, 2018.

mission becomes clearly universal in purpose. The Thomases, the Bonos, and the Ketches are pursuing mission in an urban world of need. Limitations are real, but the powerful "God of mission" has proved to be unrelenting!

Points of Wisdom

From Jason and Susan

Listening to people is a key element of incarnational urban ministry. What has surprised the Thomases is how self-proclaimed agnostics, given room to voice their questions and doubts, talk themselves into believing. A safe and welcoming environment, such as a small coffee shop, is a mercy to the big city. The environment is conducive and the listening critical to the discovery of Christ's love.

From Sal and Krystal

The time for church organizations to encourage young, post-college or graduate students with an interest in business and arts toward cities is now. A return to urban centers will begin as pastors, churches, organizations, and the younger generation are made aware of the opportunities, re-enter the urban context, live in the neighborhood, and holistically serve the common good.

From Brad And Lynn

Community is not just a good idea or a project, it occurs when people acknowledge that they need each other. As multiple ethnicities create new businesses at the Sunrise Center, share the facility, and work side-by-side, they are in a sense "forced" to model community. For the most part, these groups never intended to be *with* one another, but are now dependent on one another. In this way, "entrepreneurial success" is most transformational.

12

Risky Rescue: A *Just* Surrender

Part A

Love God, love your neighbor, Jesus said, a perfect sound bite for the ages.
But did Christ know how complicated my neighbors were? How hard they
were to love sometimes? How much easier it is to surround myself with
people who look and think and act like me, to love only myself? Yes, yes,
yes, he does, but he is polite and firm in his response. A messy, present,
incarnational love is the simplest and hardest call of all, the call that all of
us were created to follow.

~ D.L. Mayfield
Assimilate or Go Home: Notes From a Failed Missionary on Rediscovering
Faith

Today I'm aware of all the times I have said no to opportunities God has
placed before me because I think I'm not rich enough, equipped enough,
talented enough, strong enough, or crazy enough to say yes. All the times I
have mistaken good things for bad. All the times I have allowed the
opinions of an ignorant majority to guide my thinking instead of looking to
Jesus and his heart in the matter. I wonder how many times we, his
children, choose a comfortable no over a terrifying yes—the kind of yes that

will lead us to the only place we should ever long to be: in the arms of Jesus.

~ Heather Avis
The Lucky Few

Let no one be discouraged by the belief there is nothing one man or one woman can do against the enormous array of the world's ills—against misery and ignorance, injustice and violence . . . Few will have the greatness to bend history itself; but each of us can work to change a small portion of events, and in the total of all those acts will be written the history of this generation. . .

~ John F. Kennedy

The decision to do what is just in God's eyes has never been a matter of personal preference—it is more like a holy apprehension. Five years ago, I was asked by denominational leadership to create a number of networks that focused around specific interests/causes—primarily issues of social justice. The Syrian Refugee Crisis, which abruptly brought the world's attention to an unprecedented global migration, prompted the first of these networks. Like so many, I had been stirred by the news reports of violence and persecution created by a civil war. Accompanying the news reports were graphic photos, most notably of a three-year old boy's dead body washed ashore on a Turkish beach—the victim of a deadly attempt by his family to flee Syria. I read, watched, wept, and prayed—my heart was apprehended.

Others, of course, were also "apprehended" and a network of experienced refugee advocates was formed. In the ensuing years, the network has helped interested pastors and churches come alongside refugees, asylum seekers, and immigrants from a number of countries as they seek to resettle in the U.S. Gleaning from the experts, government agencies, and other non-profit organizations, the network (a.k.a. task force) offers church leaders the education, resources, and connections they need to serve well.

The Refugee Network became a template for additional networks such as the Foster Advocacy Network and the Anti Human Trafficking Network. These groups focus on the rescue of men, women, and children from various forms of trauma, exploitation, and violence. Coordinating the efforts of these groups has allowed me to rub shoulders with those who have been wholly, "holy-apprehended" by Christ. They are among the most valiant believers who surrender—risk it all—to rescue those in need of justice. "Risky Rescue" will include two chapters. The issue of human trafficking, though a category unto itself, is intrinsically linked to the exploitation of vulnerable foster children and refugee populations.

The Hardest Call of All

The scene in Luke 5:1-11 described a new dream, a new mission . . . a brand-new calling for three fishermen. Jesus climbed into Simon Peter's boat and asked him and his partners to let down the nets. Before the night was over, the nets were brimming with fish—almost enough to capsize their boat *and* the nearby boat summoned to help. I am always a bit amused at Peter's response. Seeing the enormous catch, Peter fell to his knees and said, "Master, leave. I'm a sinner and can't handle this holiness. Leave me to myself (Lk 5:8 The Message)." His words remind me of the response we often have when we are faced, maybe for the first time, with the reality that Jesus is far greater and more powerful than we understood. Sometimes it's easier not-to-know about anything or anyone that would require something more of the "sinner" in us. Sometimes it's easier to say, "Just leave me alone, Lord! I can't handle any of this!"

Coming face to face with the realities of our world is never easy, but neither is knowing that there is a holy God who *intentionally* invites us to the action. Peter, James and John were given an invitation to join Jesus as he dispensed a new kind of justice, motivated by righteousness and compassion. Though they were not fully aware of all the ramifications, these men signed on for something much bigger than themselves. The following are stories of social justice practitioners that may have rather said, "I can't handle this, Lord!" In the face of risking the unknown, Jesus assured them just as he had Peter; "There is nothing to fear. From now on you'll be fishing for men and women (Lk 5:10 The Message)." This was no longer a "catch and clean" fishing operation. It was a human "catch and release" operation. The rescue stories you are about to read are literally freeing men, women, and children to live new lives.

Rescue and Welcome: The Gosha and Seremet Stories

America, in recent history, has had a curious relationship with refugees. The latter half of the twentieth century saw waves of displaced persons seeking refuge. Each wave, regardless of ethnic origin, met with opposition from the American public and, depending on the political party in power, resettled in greater or lesser numbers. Almost two-thirds of the American population disagreed with the U.S. receiving Indochinese (boat people from Vietnam, Laos, and Cambodia) in the late seventies, and in the early eighties, almost three-quarters of U.S. citizens disagreed with the admittance of Cuban refugees. Sympathy towards ethnic Albanians from Kosovo in the late nineties was much greater—with two-thirds in favor. The latest refugee crisis found Americans almost evenly split on whether or not the U.S. had any responsibility to help Syrian refugees in the largest human-migration since World War II.[150] At the height of the crisis in 2016, over 15,000 Syrian Refugees were resettled in U.S. cities. By 2019, the number had dwindled to six-hundred and thirty-one.[151] So far, 2020 has seen zero refugees,[152] in part due to the COVID19 pandemic, but primarily as a result of the current administration's policy. Government restrictions

---

[150] Drew Desilver Pew Research, "U.S. Public Seldom Has Welcomed Refugees into Country," https://www.pewresearch.org/fact-tank/2015/11/19/u-s-public-seldom-has-welcomed-refugees-into-country/ 2015, accessed March 10, 2020.

[151] Erin Duffin Statista, "Syrian Refugee Arrival in the United States from 2011-2019," https://www.statista.com/statistics/742553/syrian-refugee-arrivals-us/) 2020, accessed March 10, 2020.

[152] Refugee Processing Center, "Admissions and Arrivals, Admissions Report 2020," https://www.wrapsnet.org/admissions-and-arrivals/ 2020, accessed June 10, 2020.

notwithstanding, the downward trend in resettlement reflects a growing opposition and perhaps a growing apathy among the American public.

The statistics tell a story of *the* nation of immigrants, once outsiders looking for a better life in a free America, now resisting that freedom for others. The numbers represent a once compassionate nation coming to the aid of the weary, tired, poor, and persecuted, now hardened to the plight of those most in need of rescue. Beyond "attitudes" and political leaning, the current climate around the refugee issue is one of unwarranted fear that dehumanizes and often villainizes those of different ethnicities, religions, or customs. The Bible, however, sets a different precedent by interlocking the Old and New Testament commands to love your neighbor, including the foreigner, stranger, or sojourner. Leviticus 19:33-34 states unequivocally, "When a foreigner resides among you in your land, do not mistreat them. The foreigner residing among you must be treated as your native-born. Love them as yourself, for you were foreigners in Egypt. I am the Lord your God (Lv 19:33-34)." Jesus adequately reinforced the Father's heart for the foreigner (alien or stranger) when he commanded us to love our neighbor (Lk 10:27) and commended those that welcomed the stranger as if they were welcoming Christ himself (Mt 25:35).

Following the biblical pattern of caring for refugees are Joe Gosha and Bethany Seremet. Individually, they have served in various capacities with several organizations--Joe for over four decades and Bethany for over a decade—living their faith by loving *all* their neighbors. With Scriptural confidence uncompromised by popular or political views, Joe and Bethany actively minister to refugee families resettled in the U.S.

Apprehended for Good

Joe and Bethany are from very different eras, but their stories have a shared theme and common passion. God has apprehended both for a lifetime of serving refugees. Service, for each, has the twists and turns of any good story, but ultimately finds them secure in their calling.

Initially, Joe was unaware of God's hand in his life decisions, but looking back, the unfolding of his life's purpose is unmistakable. Following college, he moved from Rhode Island to Minnesota and found himself temporarily living at the Minneapolis YMCA. There, at the "Y's" gym, he befriended three young Vietnamese men who enjoyed volleyball as much as he did. After getting to know one another, the boys invited Joe to dinner at their apartment. He accepted the invitation, but fear quickly replaced his enthusiasm. The apartment was located in one of Minneapolis' most dangerous neighborhoods. In addition to the location, the language barrier and, frankly, what kind of strange cuisine he might be served, Joe was intimidated! At the last minute, he decided not to show up. The boys later confronted him. Feeling terrible, Joe set a new date with his *from-another-culture* friends, and he was there as promised. As time progressed and friendship grew, the four rented an apartment together. Joe helped them with English, and they, in turn, taught Joe Vietnamese.

Joe's acquired command of the Vietnamese language led to an invitation by the Minnesota United Methodist Conference to help with the denomination's refugee program. The Indochinese, displaced by the Vietnam War, made up the largest number of refugees in the U.S. at the time. In the absence of the current Refugee Resettlement Act, volunteers and funding came primarily from churches rather than the U.S. government. People from Vietnam, Laos, and Cambodia were dependent on Voluntary Agencies (private agencies that work with the State Department to provide reception and placement services for refugees) and their church partners. Joe worked as a volunteer, helping to sponsor and temporarily house refugees, and supported himself by working in the trust department of a local bank. While excelling at his job, his interaction with Indochinese refugees was so positive, he decided to seek out a full-time job in refugee resettlement. Joe's decision led him to Los Angeles where he served as a caseworker for the International Rescue Committee, a public NGO that provides relief assistance and long-term aid to refugees. God had apprehended Joe for good—whether he was aware or not.

Bethany was a young teen sixteen years ago when she participated in a mission's outreach to Ukraine with her Christian high school. Working with orphans, street kids, and gypsies, her heart was instantly captivated. From a typical white, middle-class home, Bethany had never been exposed to such poverty and need. She would return to Ukraine, participating in the school's outreach, for her subsequent junior and senior years of high school. By the time Bethany graduated, she didn't want to do anything but "go love people." Planning to head back to her friends in the Ukraine for the foreseeable future, Bethany's mother intervened and *convinced* her to first attend college. It turned out the years of study, rather than dissuade her zeal to serve people in need, gave her newfound skills and focus. While completing a degree in communications, Bethany taught English for a language institute that catered to international businessmen. The opportunity gave her access to her students' wives, whom Bethany quickly befriended. As she helped women of varying nationalities with language skills and U.S. customs, God deepened a love for other cultures and people groups, just as he had done in Ukraine.

Bethany went on to earn a graduate degree in international politics and global economics. During her graduate studies, she was introduced to the International Justice Mission. While greatly admiring the advocacy work of IJM with victims of human-trafficking, Bethany was seeing a bigger picture of all the issues she cared about—poverty, homelessness, hunger, malnutrition, safe water, women's rights, and human trafficking—as interconnected. Her exposure abroad and at home left her unable to pick one "issue" in which to participate. With the rise of refugees in the U.S., Bethany realized she could make a sustainable difference in all of the above issues by focusing her service on refugee families. Six months before receiving her master's degree, she applied for a position at Lutheran Social Services, a Voluntary Agency (VOLAG) in New Hampshire, to help resettle refugees. Years before, serving in Ukraine, God had apprehended Bethany's heart, filling her with understanding and compassion for a culture other than her own. He had prepared her, in advance, for her present calling.

Realities and Perspective

The years to come confirmed a growing commitment to refugee resettlement. Bethany and Joe served as caseworkers, finding both rewards and difficulties present realities. On the upside, working directly with client services provided ample time to build friendships. In fact, Joe has maintained decades-long friendships with refugees and their families. He has helped newcomers assimilate to American culture, watched their children grow up, and valued them as family members. Often, the second generation considering Joe a brother, father, or grandfather.

Bethany's relationships were frequently formed over a cup of tea as she gave explanation to the endless paperwork required of refugees. Those "visits" created an atmosphere of cultural understanding, appreciation, and eventually trust. She found herself a part of the everyday life and special occasions that brought with them a plethora of wonderful—sometimes hilarious—memories. Bethany recalls having to intervene when one family roasted a chicken over an open fire . . . in the living room! Though medically unqualified, she attended the births of several refugee women, often encouraging moms and dads at a loss to understand American hospitals. One Rohingya woman, from Myanmar, hid in a hospital closet fearing the cost of the room would be more than her husband could pay!

Beyond the joy of meaningful relationships, friendships with refugees catalyzed spiritual growth, challenged perceptions, and reinforced convictions for both Bethany and Joe. Bethany says, "I stay close to the Gospels; watching how Jesus *watched* and asking myself, 'How did he act?' This I know, Jesus would be in a lifestyle of justice, open-handed with his life. This should be the norm [for his followers]. We should be living on behalf of other people."

Openhandedness with refugees has changed the way Bethany perceives ministry. Refugees taught her to listen well and retrained her instinctive need to give answers and solve problems. "Presence" became the gift that enriched both cultures. Similarly, Joe living on behalf of others, recognized life should be seen as a journey—especially in spiritual transformation. Loving and serving refugees has changed his view of God's work of conversion and discipleship. "Sometimes the longer view is more advantageous. Quick responses to the gospel are what we often see, but God doesn't require those kinds of quick responses. I see him using seed I planted forty-three years ago in the lives of the children and grandchildren of refugees." Joe readily admits, "I'm no longer so black and white, cut and dried about where *I* think people stand with God—even if they don't believe as I do. The outcome depends on God. If someone is honestly searching for God, *he* will find them."

Joe and Bethany are adamant that ministry to refugees is full of rewards, but realistically, it can also be physically and emotionally taxing. Refugee families are often relocated to a city, then later move to join relatives or communities of refugees from a particular nation. There is a dreaded sadness at the disconnect transition can bring. To remain intentional at building relationship, in spite of the inevitable relocations, isn't easy but absolutely the Christ-like choice.

There is also a physical toll. Joe found himself consistently working seventy-hour weeks at IRC, and Bethany spent many sixteen-hour days at Lutheran Social Services. The unsustainable pace led Bethany to work outside the field for a time. During that time, she led the Foursquare Refugee Network in their efforts to create a manual for refugee care and develop an interactive online class to educate pastors and leaders. Joe returned to banking and then to a brief acting career. Eventually, he served as a pastor and an immigration specialist for the Foursquare Church. At present, Joe facilitates the Foursquare Refugee Network. Currently, Bethany serves as the Director of Partnership Engagement at World Relief in Baltimore. She helps U.S. churches engage with refugees—at home and abroad—allowing them to aim locally and extend globally. Bethany is grateful to, once again, holistically focus on refugees.[153] Joe continues to

---

[153] Bethany Seremet, interview with author, August 30, 2018.

provide pro bono assistance with green card applications, serves as a volunteer among refugees in a government-housing complex, and advocates for new laws that accommodate the "stranger among us."[154]

The Bigger Risk

Advocacy on behalf of refugees is a lifelong practice of faith for Joe and Bethany. As they discover new ways to serve refugees and the church, God has been faithful to broaden their influence. Now, as never before, there is a need to educate Christ followers. According to Lifeway Research, a poll of Evangelicals revealed that while fifty-three percent were familiar with what the Bible says about how immigrants should be treated, only twelve percent say the Bible influences their views on immigration. The media was rated as one of the highest influencers.[155] Bethany, in a recent webinar, observed the limited viewpoints offered by media on this issue. The church, however, has the distinct advantage of Scripture that is holistic and comprehensive regarding our engagement with and treatment of refugees and immigrants. Remembering that Jesus himself was a refugee (Mt 2:13-18) will help Christ followers love their neighbors—those religiously and ethnically different from us (Lu 10:25-37)—and recognize the inherent dignity and worth of every person God created.[156] Joe would remind us to keep human beings that need assistance a priority rather than a ministry target, viewing people as humans created by God—embracing them as neighbors and our friends. To live in such a way transforms us into disciples that place service above self.

Bethany Seremet and Joe Gosha have learned that the bigger risk is to *not* serve, *not* love, *not* befriend, and *not* advocate on behalf of refugees and/or vulnerable immigrants. To do so, would risk the many ways in which their own lives have been enriched. Most importantly, to not obey God's

---

[154] Joe Gosha, interview with author, August 8, 2018.

[155] Lifeway Research, "Evangelical View on Immigration Report," http://lifewayresearch.com/wp-content/uploads/2015/03/Evangelical-Views-on-Immigration-Report.pdf 2015, accessed April 10, 2020.

[156] Beth Seremet, "Leading Your Congregation to Welcome the Stranger in a Politically Complex Environment," 2020.

commands would risk the large numbers of refugee lives transformed through Christ's love . . . *and* the many *yet to be* transformed by his great grace.

Rescue and Family: The Cooke Story

A mark of true Christianity is to care for orphans. James 1:27 affirms, "Religion that God our Father accepts as pure and faultless is this: to look after orphans and widows in their distress and to keep oneself from being polluted by the world." As foster children in the U.S. number in the hundreds of thousands—four-hundred and twenty-four thousand plus as of 2018[157]—Christ-followers are responding to modern-day "orphans" and the systems that support their care. Among those respondents are Mike and Molly Cooke.

Mike and Molly are the pastors of a now sizeable church in a small community located just outside Portland, Oregon. Their appointment to the once struggling church coincided with a personal struggle to become parents. The church and their family have grown side by side and resulted in an unexpected community engagement with foster children, foster families, and social services.

Adding to the Family

The Cooke's, after a long season of medical intervention to conceive, decided adoption was their best option for children. Mike, in line with his character, created a spreadsheet of every adoption agency he could find. He included both international and domestic adoptions, private and open adoptions, the adoption of bi-racial children—and the cost of each process. In some cases, the cost was prohibitive, but Mike and Molly trusted God to find a way.

Prior to beginning the formal adoption process, Molly had received word from a friend regarding two foster children, a sibling set, who were "legally

---

[157] Annie E. Casey Foundation, "What Is Foster Care, Updated April 14, 2020," https://www.aecf.org/topics/foster-care/ 2020, accessed April 30, 2020.

free" for adoption. Molly immediately contacted her friend, but both quickly realized the impossibility of completing the necessary steps in a long qualification process. The Cooke's had not considered fostering children, because their goal was to have a child, or hopefully children, become a permanent part of their family. Though the lengthy paperwork, classes, and required home study would prohibit this particular adoption, they were grateful to learn of the "foster-to-adopt" program as another possible option.

Mike and Molly promptly contacted Oregon's Department of Human Services (DHS) and began the certification process. The Cookes were open to adopt children of a different ethnicity from their own, and now in their thirties, they were also receptive to the idea of older children. Their openness made them desirable candidates. It was just eight months later that Mike and Molly adopted a sibling set, four and five-year old brothers. Four years later, they received another sibling set—this time a brother and sister. Three months after children three and four, a young boy fostered by fellow church staff members became eligible for adoption. Molly recalls their friends and coworkers painfully sharing the news that they were unable to become their foster son's "forever family." Suddenly, Mike blurted out, "Maybe . . . we'll adopt him!" The Cookes close personal and work relationship with the family had given them, and especially Mike, a unique bond with the little guy. In a process that can take up to two years, the Cookes received their fifth child in just two and a half weeks!

Almost a decade later, as the two oldest Cooke children drew close to high school graduation, Mike asked Molly how she would feel about foster parenting rather than fostering-to-adopt. The house was too empty . . . too quiet. With Molly's agreement, they signed up to begin foster parenting classes and received their first emergency placement, a fourteen-year-old girl, two months later. Six months later, they received another emergency placement, a nine-year-old boy. Unforeseen by the Cookes, their second official "foster" son became available for adoption—and, of course, they were anxious to add yet another family member. Molly jokes that their desire to adopt children of different ethnicities has *almost* been fulfilled. The oldest two look just like them—white and light-haired; the second set have Hispanic roots; the third is a vivid red-head (perhaps some Irish heritage); and the last adopted is African American. "All I need now is my Asian 'china doll,'" says Molly. It seems there might be room for one more in the Cooke household.

Serving Social Services

Making room for kids in their home caused an "organic explosion" of foster care in their church. Within a month of Mike and Molly's first adoption through the Foster Care System, members of their church began applying to become foster parents or to adopt. Molly, tongue in cheek, says, "The Lord never kills just one bird with a stone." In this case, the old adage has proved abundantly true. A natural progression began as the church moved to a new location . . . directly across from their local DHS (Department of Human Services) office, which oversees Foster Care in their county. The church facility was built with the city in mind. Several government agencies, the school district, and DHS utilize the church space as their own. In fact, Mike and Molly, supplied a church key to DHS so they could readily use the building for parental visitations—a place with a less sterile atmosphere that put families at ease.

The provision of space, however, was just a first step in a relationship between the church and the city that has emerged over the last seventeen years. Mike, Molly, and their church have earned an uncommon trust that works for the common good. In part, the 2008 economic crisis created a need for resources that the church was willing to provide. But with or without a crisis, Molly states, "Before *missional* was a buzzword in the church, we wanted our congregation to change the perception of why churches exist in a city. As far as we were concerned, we were there to serve the city."

That service continues as Columbia River Foursquare (CRF) opens its doors to any and all county agencies, but their ardent participation with DHS has resulted in passionate support on a number of levels. The church regularly holds banquets to honor social workers and provide them with a much-needed night out. They continue to provide visitation space for families, making sure both children, foster parents, and biological parents have everything they need to make the visit successful. Countywide trainings for trauma-informed care, in conjunction with Portland-based therapists, are hosted to better prepare foster families and social workers. In addition, CRF's children's pastor serves as the director of Every Child—an organization that brings together needed services from businesses, churches, and the government. The church hosts and staffs Foster Parent's Night Out—a four-hour respite program for foster parents. CRF is active in bridging the gap between social workers and foster parents, aiding foster families after a placement leaves, and creating greater communication between all the entities involved. Each of these services have evolved over the years. Molly is quick to note that CRF is just one piece of the puzzle. Their entire community—each church, each agency, and each program is a necessary component to seeing every child placed in a family. She adds, "This is a *solvable* issue."

Solutions have come with greater awareness. Mike and Molly's adoptions through Foster Care provided first-hand knowledge of the system. However, it was their role as foster parents that allowed them a more comprehensive view of present needs. They became more informed of good and bad legislation (or good legislation not enforced!) surrounding the issue. When a child they fostered faced trauma-induced behavioral issues, Molly discovered a myriad of available services. She tenaciously pursued resources in her community and everything the city of Portland and the state of Oregon had to offer. Molly comments, "When I realized there was help out there, that there were options for help and healing . . . that there was hope . . . it unleashed the beast in me!" Molly persevered and found a therapeutic program that included school supports alongside psychiatric and trauma-informed care. After completion of the program, Free Appropriate Public Education (FAPE) enacted by the state of Oregon, guaranteed education at a school equipped to offer therapy supports. The experience of fostering a child with special needs was motivation for Molly to practically connect other foster parents with services from every sector of the city—private, public, and religious. The discovery of resources enhanced the link between serving well and being well served.

A Worthy Endeavor

Molly is quick to encourage foster advocacy and adoption. However, she knows that foster or adoptive parents will face inevitable challenges. Personally, fears arose when she and Mike initially began to adopt through the foster system. Molly now chuckles at some of her unreasonable fears . . . *what if the child I receive grows up to be an addict, a psychopath, or a criminal* . . . or *what if this child changes my relationship with Mike or our nieces and nephews?* After walking through six adoptions, she echoes the truth spoken by family and friends: There are no guarantees with adoptive children, *and* there are no guarantees with biological children! Every child, regardless of the problems he or she faces, *needs* love. Each new addition to a family will bring a new dynamic—something God uses for the growth and benefit of biological, adoptive, *and* foster families.

Likewise, congregations can face apprehensions. Churches that open their doors, hearts, and budgets may experience additional wear and tear on their building, staff, and volunteers. They may be stretched with time and monetary commitments. Molly encourages:

> Each church is unique. Each community is unique. When
> exposed to what others are doing, rather than be
> overwhelmed, find where it is God has given you favor.
> Detail the ministry to the DNA of your church. There are no
> cookie-cutter programs when it comes to foster advocacy.
> Listen with interest, then follow your specific calling.

Perhaps there is no better way to describe this worthy journey than knowing that God sees in all directions. Molly recalls a reassuring spiritual picture in which she was standing on a city street, facing a tall building, while Jesus was positioned at the cross street. Her view was limited, but Christ had a *full* view from all sides. Looking back and forth, he simply said, "Oh, Molly, it's going to be good!" Grateful for God's gracious encouragement, both Mike and Molly pray that individuals and churches will take a chance on today's orphans.

They pray entire communities will hear God speak, "Oh . . . it's going to be so good."[158]

Welcome and Family Matter

Each of us, adopted by the Father, served by Christ, and comforted by the Holy Spirit, experience a joyous welcome to our new "forever" family. Joe, Bethany, Molly and Mike, with Christ-like character, serve the vulnerable among us. They are examples of the way in which all of us have opportunities to welcome strangers to our land . . . to our churches . . . to our cities . . . and to our homes. For refugees and foster children, a new home means protection and shelter from the harsh realities they might otherwise face. The following chapter will provide additional insights into the protections needed for refugees and foster children who find themselves vulnerable to exploitation, especially in the urban centers of the world.

Points of Wisdom

From Joe

Joe refers to himself as "the love on, demonstration guy." He is the absent family member [to refugees] . . . the dad, grandfather, older brother. Joe would encourage others, that if Christ is alive in you, there is no agenda needed. So many of the refugees he's befriended are now followers of Jesus, of whom he says, "I could not have preached them into the kingdom." Instead, Joe loved them in!

From Bethany

When it comes to refugees or vulnerable immigrant populations, the church hesitates, fearful that they might do something unlawful and therefore neglect God's command to be subject to governing authorities. Bethany reminds us that we do not need to choose between obedience to the

---

[158] Molly Cooke, interview by author, August 16, 2018.

laws of the land and loving our neighbors. We can do both. There is no legal issue with engaging immigrants (even those undocumented). While we cannot employ an undocumented worker, there are no legal ramifications for providing English classes, day care services, ministering in asylee detention centers, feeding new friends . . . or showing hospitality to those within our borders.

From Molly

Molly encourages Christ-followers that their communities will trust a church that has offered more than words. In times of need or crisis, a city looks for those with a reputation of action and sacrifice. Foster care across the U.S. is facing a crisis. Let's give them reason to trust us. Let's show, not just tell, the gospel with our actions and sacrifices on behalf of children.

13

Risky Rescue: A *Just* Surrender

Part B

Rescue and Restoration: The Mercer, Belles, and Russell Stories

"Human trafficking is one of the most heinous crimes on Earth. Right now traffickers are robbing a staggering 24.9 million people of their freedom and basic human dignity—that's roughly three times the population of New York City." These words open the U.S. Department of State 2019 Trafficking in Persons Report.[159] The report addresses an ever-growing "business" that exploits women, men, and children as labor or sex slaves. This form of modern-day slavery exists worldwide, but the U.S. along with Mexico and the Philippines was ranked one of the world's worst places for human trafficking in 2018.[160] Within the United States:

> Populations . . . vulnerable to human trafficking include:
> children in the child welfare and juvenile justice systems,
> including foster care; runaway and homeless youth;
> unaccompanied foreign national children without lawful

---

[159] U.S. State Department, "2019 Trafficking in Persons Report," https://www.state.gov/reports/2019-trafficking-in-persons-report/, 2019, accessed May 4, 2020.

[160] James Pasley Business Insider, "20 Staggering Facts About Human Trafficking in the U.S.," https://www.businessinsider.com/human-trafficking-in-the-us-facts-statistics-2019-7, 2019, accessed May 4, 2020.

immigration status; American Indians and Alaska Natives, particularly women and girls; individuals with drug addictions; migrant laborers, including undocumented workers and participants in visa programs for temporary workers; foreign national domestic workers in diplomatic households; persons with limited English proficiency; persons with disabilities; LGBTI individuals; and participants in court-ordered substance use diversion programs. Advocates reported a growing trend of traffickers targeting victims with disabilities and an increase in the use of online social media platforms to recruit and advertise victims of human trafficking. Some U.S. citizens engage in child sex tourism in foreign countries.[161]

Regarding vulnerable foster children, the New York Times noted, in a 2019 article, that fifty percent of traumatized foster youth have been in the foster care system.[162] The U.S. Office of the Inspector General, casting a larger net, reported in 2019 that six years previous "up to 90% of children who were victims of sex trafficking had been involved with *child welfare services*, which include foster care."[163] A new study to track U.S. states' trafficking prevention progress will take place in 2021.

Outside the U.S., on the international scene, refugees are particularly at risk. Again, the U.S. State Department candidly reports:

Camps for refugees and internally displaced persons are prime targets for traffickers. The concentration of vulnerable, displaced people, combined with a lack of security, services, and oversight typically found in such camps, make them ideal locations for

---

[161] Department, U.S. State, 492.

[162] Rikha Sharma Rani New York Times, "Homes to Heal Trafficked Children," https://www.nytimes.com/2019/06/19/opinion/foster-child-trafficking.html 2019, accessed June 1, 2020.

[163] Office of Inspector General U.S. Department of Health and Human Services, "State's Prevention of Child Sex Trafficking in Foster Care," https://www.oig.hhs.gov/reports-and-publications/workplan/summary/wp-summary-0000396.asp, 2019, accessed June 15, 2020.

traffickers to operate. In long-standing camps, traffickers are able to build relationships with corrupt camp officials, and establish trafficking rings.[164]

The trafficking rings extend beyond given camp locations. With promises for a better life in another country, human smugglers deliver their "customers" to a life of servitude. End Slavery Now, an anti-trafficking organization clarifies:

> While something may begin as human smuggling—paying a person to move you or your family across a border—it can sometimes end in human trafficking. Some smugglers have used debts incurred during transit as a way to enslave people, others have used brute force. Displaced people, both internally and externally, often face dire poverty. People in poverty, and without adequate community or family networks, are vulnerable to human trafficking and susceptible to human trafficking snares and schemes.[165]

Traffickers seek out the most vulnerable, but the defenseless aren't always those we would suspect to be at risk. In the U.S., "many . . . young victims are runaways or foster children, others are from what would be considered 'good' families and have been lured or coerced into human trafficking by clever predators."[166] The wide range of victims add to the abhorrence of those who participate in such crimes against fellow humans. The repulsive nature of this issue could make it easy for Christ-followers to walk away in disbelief, ignoring the reality. That is not the case for modern day abolitionists and the organizations they represent. Among those working to combat human trafficking in the U.S. and abroad are Mike Mercer, Nita Belles, and Vanessa Russell. Each came to believe that the one thing they couldn't do, is do nothing.

---

[164] Department, U.S. State, 32.

[165] End Slavery Now, "Human Trafficking, Refugees and Displaced Persons: What Terms to Use " http://www.endslaverynow.org/blog/articles/human-trafficking-refugees-and-displaced-persons-what-terms-to-use, 2015, accessed June 15, 2020.

[166] Nita Belles, "In Our Backyard : Human Trafficking in America and What We Can Do to Stop It," 2015. 24.

Awareness Equals Action

Mike, Nita, and Vanessa came to a place of awareness through circumstances, personal history, fresh theological views, heart-change, and a God-directive. They were not always certain of the how, when, or where, but the *what* was never questioned as they actively engaged anti-trafficking activity.

Mike's Beginning

Mike, a staff pastor at a mega-church in Beaverton (metro Portland), Oregon, came home one day to find his wife, Kymra, unnerved by an episode of the *OPRAH* show. She had just watched a one-hour special on human trafficking and was particularly alarmed by the volume of children affected. Kymra looked at her youth pastor husband and uttered these words, "I think you are supposed to do something about it!" The words sunk deep, but Mike had no idea *how* to do anything about such a widespread and complex issue. Already in the preparation stage of planting a church in Austin, Texas, the Mercers thought the answer might be to begin a non-profit in conjunction with the church plant. However, before any concrete details could be planned, Hurricane Katrina hit the Gulf Coast. Mike's heart was immediately touched by the devastation—particularly for the poor affected by the storm. The church Mike served had the same visceral response and was prepared to help. Just 24 hours after Mike learned of the need, the senior pastor requested that he lead relief efforts in the Gulf.

Relief ministry might have seemed like a detour from his church planting and non-profit aspirations had it not been that, months before Mike was aware of the prevalence of human-trafficking, and well before Katrina, he had been reading the Bible, in his words, "more naked." He was beginning to see beyond evangelical filters to the depth of God's heart for the poor, the victim, and the exploited. He struggled to discover where and to whom he was called. His reality was serving upper middle-class students, which was good and right, but God seemed to be pulling him in a different direction. As Mike said yes to ministry in the Gulf, the issue of *what he could do* was settled on several fronts. To his surprise, the role not only aligned his heart and mission before God, it prepared him for his eventual position as the founder and director of Compassion First—a non-profit for the rescue and restoration of trafficking survivors.

Nita's Beginning

Nita was pursuing a degree in theology, at Bakke Graduate University, when one of her courses required her to read several books on human trafficking. Though Nita herself was a survivor of domestic violence, she could not fathom the devastation and destruction of trafficking. Her immediate response was to ask, "God, what do you want *me* to do?" God's reply was, "I want you to write a book." Nita was NOT happy. Though a graduate student, she never considered herself academic. In fact, as much as she loved learning, she disliked writing. In obedience, Nita followed God's directive. The result was a book uniquely focused on human trafficking in the U.S. as told through the stories of survivors. Nita wrote from a Christian perspective and hoped her book would awaken the church to the crisis right in our backyard. However, her audience became government organizations, law enforcement agencies, schools, social services . . . and "real people" directly affected by modern-day slavery. The wider acceptance of the book led to a revised and expanded book, acquired by a major publisher. *In Our Backyard: Human Trafficking in the U.S. and How to Stop It* subsequently became the basis for the non-profit, In Our Backyard, that works for broader awareness in communities through education and legislation.

Vanessa's Beginning

Vanessa candidly says, "I was called to this [anti human trafficking ministry] before I was born!" Her family history included a grandmother who was exploited for sex, became pregnant by a "buyer," and gave birth to Vanessa's father. Family saga aside, Vanessa had a rough life before Christ intervened. As a child, she was in foster care for a time. As an adult, she experienced an abusive marriage and, after leaving her abuser, faced life as a single parent. Things changed when she committed her life to Christ at age 30. Vanessa was drawn to at-risk youth—or "opportunity youth"—and began dance classes at her church for children and teens. She recalls how real human trafficking became when one of her 15-year old dance students was raped and sold for sex. Vanessa began a relentless search for the girl. In the process, she became fully inculcated in the issue, learning about a level of exploitation she was unaware existed. She couldn't sleep at night. The hip-hop song, *How to Love,* by Lil Wayne,[167] played over and over in her head. Her heart was completely broken. In fact, Vanessa prayed that God would break her heart for what broke his. She, honestly, felt she had no choice. Vanessa says, "I could NOT, not do something." She began a street outreach to rescue survivors—a precursor to the non-profit Love Never Fails which offers housing, counseling, and job training to those who have been trafficked.

Entering the Non-Profit World

Finding a unique contribution among the plethora of anti-trafficking non-profits is a significant discovery. While collaboration and joint projects remain an unequivocal factor for survival and effectiveness, proximity and specific services can help determine organizational focus, aid in the creation of programs, and fully engage a community of non-profits.

Survivor After-Care

Mike learned a great deal while serving in the Gulf. Early in the process, an elderly woman who had served as a procurement specialist for a humanitarian aid organization, Northwest Medical Teams, contacted Mike's office . . . repeatedly. The eighty-six-year-old's calls and visits were "put off" by his office staff. When Mike finally granted her a meeting, he unexpectedly became the recipient of this servant-leader's wisdom and connections. Ruth was able to obtain substantial funding to begin work in the Gulf. However, her greatest contribution was the refinement of Mike's "I-don't know-what-I'm-

---

[167] Lil Wayne, "How to Love," Tha Carter IV, https://www.bing.com/videos/search?q=how+to+love+lil+wayne&view=detail&mid=3225073 A1AC37FCE34123225073A1AC37FCE3412&FORM=VIRE0&ru=%2fsearch%3fq%3dhow%2bto %2blove%2blil%2bwayne%26form%3dAPMCS1%26PC%3dAPMC, , accessed April 15, 2020.

doing-but-I-think-we-can-strategy" to make friends, recruit volunteers, and rebuild houses.

The rebuilding of homes in Mississippi was an ominous project. Operating by invitation and with a commitment to competency training, Mike sought out the leaders of non-profits already serving the need. Habitat for Humanity, Samaritan's Purse, and the Salvation Army were present and making effective contributions. He hired several college students with grants provided by AmeriCorps, and then promptly obtained UMCORP (United Methodist Committee on Relief) management training in disaster relief to adequately prepare them for the task. Competent volunteers, grants, and cooperation resulted in the creation of a "village" that housed volunteers from various organizations for the next thirty months; the re-building of 45 homes for widows, single mothers, the aging, and disabled; an ongoing disaster relief ministry for the Foursquare denomination; and the launch of Compassion First as the managing entity of the work in the Gulf. Mike adamantly states that his competency was acquired— "and the beginning of competency is to know what you don't know."

The formation of Compassion First became a bridge to the current anti-trafficking movement. Mike duplicated the approach used for disaster relief. He began by asking questions of government and non-profits. He traveled to D.C. to meet with the State Department. He asked for an hour of time with Salvation Army, World Hope Int., IJM (International Justice Mission), FAAST (Faith Alliance Against Slavery and Trafficking), World Vision, and World Relief. He asked each, "Is there room for us? What do you need?" Most responded positively, but Mike's conversation with IJM Vice President, Shawn Whitten, brought to light the unique, often unmet, need for survivor "after care." IJM works primarily with police and the courts to curtail trafficking, and they viewed this as a prime opportunity. As Mike and Shawn continued their discussion, both noted increased trafficking in disaster zones. Shawn stated that he was personally aware of girls trafficked following the 2004 Tsunami which affected several nations bordering the Indian Ocean—including Indonesia.

The mention of Indonesia was significant for Mike. Prior to his meeting with IJM, he had attended a denominational convention in Chicago. At the conference, a welcome was extended to an Indonesian church organization joining their ranks. Mike and Kymra could not figure out why their hearts were so stirred. Years later, Indonesia would become the hub of their anti-trafficking ministry and the location of two homes for survivors. Aided by the Foursquare Church of Indonesia, after-care has become Compassion First's primary focus. Mike once thought this aspect of anti-trafficking was "pansy" work. He has learned since that working with the seemingly more important legal issues is the *easy* part. Though the organization is involved in rescue and advocacy, after-care requires greater longevity, commitment, and resources; and it is the "piece" that produces restored, whole lives.

Public Awareness

Nita founded In Our Backyard (IOB) with the objective of making the trafficking issue known, understood, and detectable. Often relegated as an international and/or big city problem, the activity of traffickers in the U.S. had gone largely without notice—especially by the church. Nita saw the need for education in our churches, schools, police departments, and public and private institutions in both large and small communities. Aware and alert citizens are key to the end of human trafficking.

The newly founded non-profit quickly discovered that they were more effective working with others. Nita was active with OATH (Oregonians Against Trafficking Humans) and was often invited to speak at civic and church events. IOB set out to "link arms" across America to fight human trafficking. In working with other non-profits, Nita learned to look for points of agreement, for partners with like values, and to let love lead the way with patience. Non-profits often feel they are competing for the same funds. In reality, each one has a part to play, and close observation reveals a pattern of an organization's strength and character. Nita began asking, "How does this organization get the job done?" and "Is the trafficking survivor the most important person in the equation?"

Those questions have helped IOB find viable partners in a number of sectors. Instruction and awareness training at schools led to the formation of Teens Against Trafficking, a comprehensive presentation to educate middle and high school students in Oregon where IOB is located. Freedom Stickers were developed in conjunction with the National Human Trafficking Hotline to place the hotline number in public restrooms—the safest place for trafficking victims to call for help. The stickers are currently utilized in all fifty states and documented recoveries have resulted. IOB created the CSAT (Convenience Stores Against Trafficking) program, and have trained Convenience Store and Gas Station staff and employees to be aware of the signs of trafficking. At this writing, more than twenty thousand convenience stores, along with national and state leaders, have effectively partnered with CSAT. In addition, IOB trains law enforcement, probation, and parole officers to recognize trafficking activity. For over a decade, IOB has been present at Super Bowl—just one example of large sporting events that draw traffickers—to train law enforcement and social service workers, aid in the arrest of traffickers, canvas local businesses, and disperse flyers of missing children. In addition, IOB is continually involved in the support of legislation that protects victims and prosecutes traffickers.

Education, Mentorship, and Housing

Vanessa's search for her 15-year old student ended well. As an IT specialist, she located the missing girl via internet ads. Delving into lengthy research, Vanessa followed the trail and then provided what she found to the district attorney and police. From the ads, the police were able to locate the teenager and subsequently arrest her for activity unrelated to "prostitution." She was placed in an out-of-state program for a year and eventually returned to California. Vanessa was able to connect the teen survivor with an older survivor, by whom she was formally adopted through foster care.

The story of Vanessa's student goes far deeper than a happy ending. During the eight-month search and a lengthy post-rescue period, she looked into options for her young friend. A newly established residential program, New Day for Children, was one possibility. However, the funding for the home was based on the limited support of churches and would require more than Vanessa, a single, working mother could raise. With her pastor's permission, she made a plea to her church that brought in more than enough finances to secure a bed. In the end, the student decided against the program and Vanessa returned the funds. However, as a positive consequence of the fund-raising venture, the congregation had come face-to-face with the issue of human trafficking. Vanessa discovered people cared and wanted to help! Blessed by the overwhelming interest, the idea of a non-profit was introduced. She brought the concept to her pastor, and not only did he think it was a good plan, he suggested the church serve as a fiscal sponsor.

Shortly after the offer of sponsorship, Vanessa held a meeting of those interested in helping launch Love Never Fails (LNF). Their goal was to rescue the "one" because God was *not* okay with even one person being exploited. With that in mind, those present formed groups around the three areas—education, mentorship, and housing. Vanessa chose the specific topics after conferring with her "rescued" dance student. Each group presented a natural leader. Love Never Fails soon began mentoring survivors, providing prevention education for local schools, and moving toward residential care. Regarding the latter, LNF has helped house young survivors since 2011 by working with several partner organizations. Currently, plans are underway to open a new LNF residential facility by the close of 2020. A team of trauma-informed specialists is ready to aid in the restoration of survivors, and professional training for sustainable jobs remains a priority.

Tenacious Humility

Abolitionists seem to require a remarkable mix of resolute conviction—to the point of dogged determination—and tender humility rendered in a servant spirit. Perhaps both are necessary when confronting an "industry" that makes such an enormous amount of money while exploiting the lives of the vulnerable. Based on 2015 findings by the United Nations International Labor Organization, the Human Trafficking Center reports that over one-hundred and fifty billion dollars are generated worldwide each year through labor and sex trafficking. Close to a hundred billion dollars, or two-thirds of the profits, are related to sexual exploitation.[168] Anti-trafficking workers need a tremendous will to pushback on systems that support the illegal industry of human slavery, in all its forms, while graciously serving survivors. They need persistence when educating the church and public entities. They need unpretentious honesty when reporting to donors.

Strength Under Fire

Mike states, "Our (CF's) early story was so difficult . . . so hard, that we should have quit." Once established in Indonesia, Compassion First faced internal and external struggle. The month-over-month income wasn't sufficient. At one point, the organization was running so low on funds they felt lucky to survive. They weren't able to hire enough staff, and the staff they had were not proficient in therapeutic trauma-informed care.

The shortages within the organization were challenging, but it was the mounting external forces that proved most formidable. "We felt like we kicked a hornet's nest of corruption. The human rights violations were egregious. The courts were flipping cases onto survivors, imprisoning them, and then reporting to the global community that they were fighting trafficking." Mike took the story to their one ally—a local newspaper. Buying space, he reported the dealings of the police and the court system. The U.S. State Department noticed the story, and representing the department's concern, Mike wrote to the police chief letting him know he wouldn't hesitate to pass along the misinformation the chief was contributing to the Trafficking Persons Report. "I will make you famous, whether you do the right thing or not," Mike boldly penned. Suddenly, everything calmed and there was renewed peace for CF.

The settling of circumstances came, but not before Mike and his staff were made acutely aware of outright demonic opposition. One of their security guards was killed, a CF social worker was raped, and the organization's lawyer came home one night to find his house filled with snakes. During this time,

---

[168] Human Trafficking Center, "The Profits Made from Human Trafficking," accessed May 4, 2020

Mike attended a global council meeting for the denomination. When asked about CF's progress, he honestly reported that the non-profit had only one girl in the after-care program. He followed the unglamorous statistic with this: "We are so enamored by numbers, but the metrics of heaven is found in names." He shared the story behind the one name. In the next two years, CF raised a million dollars and they have never since operated below that financial benchmark.

Ten years later, CF has sixty-five employees—with whom Mike says he is "head-over-heals" in love. The culture at their offices in Beaverton, OR and onsite in East Java, North Sulawesi, and Bali includes Catholics, Muslims, mainline Protestants, and Pentecostals—all with a heart to end trafficking. The Christian mission and emphasis remains a priority and is well known among staff members; but for those still on journey, their present faith is respected. "Culture eats strategy for breakfast," is one of Mike's favorite witticisms. And the culture at CF is one of loving relationships as they bring the strength of experience and the gift of diverse backgrounds to the table in order to end trafficking.

Surrounded by Prayer

Nita's experience has taught her that typecasting victims is a mistake. Never was this fact more obvious than during her anti-trafficking work at the 2013 Super Bowl. Nita and a team of volunteers helped two college girls narrowly escape being picked up by traffickers. The under-aged Tulane University students were out for a good time as they celebrated (with alcohol) Super Bowl in New Orleans. Consequently, they found themselves at a nice bar, but near a seedy backstreet lined with pimps and victims. Fortunately, for the girls, Nita and her friends ran out of gas on the same street after their GPS led them astray. The mistake allowed them to observe the activity and the girls' frightened reaction to the unwanted advances of traffickers. Once AAA rescued Nita and her party, they were able to intervene and take the girls back to their dorm.

God's grace—and most likely the prayer of a parent or grandparent— kept these young women from becoming a statistic. Nita commented, "As we drove away from the Tulane campus, I was reminded that the fight we are in to stop human trafficking is real, and that traffickers are not selective about their victims. Any vulnerable person will do. This game is about traffickers making money."[169] In this instance, there was a happy ending with lessons learned, but Nita warns that even with a car full of experienced anti-traffickers on the spot, the standard procedure would entail police intervention. "This type of work is very dangerous and should not be undertaken without prearranged cooperation with specific law enforcement agencies and an agreed protocol of how you will cooperate with them."[170] Nita acknowledges, that though her organization has a role to play in the recovery of victims, the number of rescues and arrests are heavily dependent on law enforcement—a protection for which she is exceedingly grateful.

Protections are necessary on a number of fronts. Convinced that trafficking can be stopped, Nita also knows the personal toll is great. Hours of research to locate perpetrators takes IOB staff to places on the internet most of us would be offended to "surf." Images can be difficult to erase from the mind's eye, creating emotional turmoil. Compassion fatigue overtakes those who connect with survivors. Advocating for better legislation, just treatment of survivors, and convictions for traffickers can be an endless and thankless job—at times leaving the advocate disheartened or hopeless. The constant need for funds can create financial insecurity for the activist and the organization. The physical, emotional, and spiritual stakes are high. Nita and IOB rely on dedicated prayer. A prayer team, consisting of people Nita can trust with absolute candor and honesty, has developed over the years. When things get tough, she has those she can call at any time to support her and IOB in prayer. Nita credits the prayer team with her sanity! The boldness to confront the darkness of trafficking is found in the deferential request for prayer.

---

[169] Belles 153.
[170] Ibid.

The "Inner" Mama Bear

Friends have described Vanessa as a "Mama Bear" when it comes to finding trafficked girls. In the early street outreaches of LNF, she was talking with a girl whom she judged to be a teen, when two men pulled to the curb and began nudging the girl toward their car. Vanessa was stunned that this was happening right in front of her as the girl was forcibly pushed into the car. The team working the streets that day, about forty volunteers, immediately gathered in a nearby vacant lot and began to pray. A police car happened by, and Vanessa shared with the officer what had just happened. Ironically, when the local businesses (mostly liquor and convenience stores) saw the police talking to the group, they suddenly turned their lights off and closed their doors. A few minutes later, the girl was returned to the exact spot she had been taken. The police discovered the young woman was a missing minor from California's Central Valley. The LNF volunteers and the police surmised that the activity of the traffickers was well known in the area. They also suspicioned that one of the businesses had called the traffickers and informed them that the police were "on to them" . . . *and* that there were plenty of witnesses. The girl was not worth shutting down their entire operation. She *was* worth Vanessa activating her inner "Mama Bear!"

Vanessa discovered, through this incident and the development of LNF, the gifts God placed in her life for the very purpose of restoring survivors. "I didn't realize how strong of a prophetic voice I had." The gift of leadership was readily identified, but Vanessa was coming to grips with the fact that God could trust her with his voice or instruction as she took a step forward in faith. Her obedience has deepened her prayer life, her grasp of the Word and, most importantly, an ability to lead with wisdom. As an executive for a tech company, Vanessa had a position of influence, but her newfound strength was found in a humble dependence on God for both calling and direction.

Recently, that direction included Vanessa's resignation from an executive position and salary in order to more fully concentrate her time at LNF. Yet another step of obedience has opened doors to a rich array of programs that create opportunities for survivors and at-risk youth. In addition to the housing and mentorship so close to the LNF vision, programs such as Workforce Development and IT Biz have connected with Alameda County's "AC Hire Program." Corporate sponsors such as Wells Fargo, Cisco Systems, along with a myriad of community partners and volunteers, have sustained and enriched the programs. LNF also teamed with 3 Strands Global and Frederick Douglass Family Initiatives to form PROTECT, an educational and trafficking prevention program for children working in partnership with the California Office of the Attorney General. In addition, LNF established the Look 4 Me Program to enlist private investigators, off-duty law enforcement personnel, and justice-oriented community members to organize searches and distribute missing persons' flyers.

The above-mentioned programs, among others, are driven by Vanessa's tenacious spirit and the equally bold spirit of the LNF staff. The ability to search out partners and sponsors allows them to serve survivors and their community with "gifts" they didn't know were present. Vanessa brings out the Mama Bear . . . and the Papa Bear . . . that organizations and individuals were not aware they possessed.

Rescued and Restored

The anti-trafficking efforts of Mike, Nita, Vanessa and their organizations have resulted in the freedom of many who might otherwise have remained in the grip of their exploiters. The tactics of traffickers in the urban centers of the world, refugee camps, or "small-town" America are now broadly known due to the growing number of non-profits effectively addressing the issue. Those most vulnerable are more readily finding the help, support, and services they need. Much like the stories of Joe, Bethany, and Molly from the previous chapter, these have surrendered to a "Jesus-justice" that returns our cities and communities to places of welcome and restoration. They accepted Christ's invitation to the action—to justice motivated by righteousness and compassion.

Points of Wisdom

From Mike

"CF has learned two things: Only work where you are invited, and invite Jesus to everything." Mike's staff *looks* for *any* reason to pray and invite Christ. Working among a majority Muslim population, they have found a receptiveness to prayer and experienced many answered prayers. "It seems God goes where he is invited and he is welcome among the poor—regardless of their religion." Mike backs up the persistent invitation, noting the key theological truth in the gospel story of the wedding at Cana is not the miracle, but the fact that Jesus and the disciples were invited. The miraculous follows an invitation.

From Nita

Churches can be a healing place for survivors. However, far too often survivors are viewed as prostitutes or sex addicts. Nita suggests that we relearn how to weep with those who weep. She suggests that Christ-followers allow human trafficking to become *human* by putting a face to the issue. "Get to know a person whose life has been adversely affected and look for ways to walk beside them through the ups and downs, showing them respect and love."

From Vanessa

Vanessa's opportunity to serve trafficked persons came at a most inopportune time. A more recent Christ-follower, she was working through the after-effects of an abusive marriage and processing a messy divorce, raising two children on her own, and working a full-time job in IT. The needs of the vulnerable are not always convenient, which is why it's so important to listen to God's heart and respond to his direction. On the other side of a successful non-profit, Vanessa says, "I guess I was only half-crazy!"

Conclusion

The City Story Continues With Us

What a God! His road stretches straight and smooth.
Every God-direction is road-tested.
Everyone who runs toward him makes it.
Psalm 18:30 (The Message Bible)

Vision and mission are never solo endeavors. To see the cities of the world transformed by the love of Christ, it will take all of us working together. We will need to resist systemic brokenness while, at the same time, resisting our own passivity and indifference. We will need greater compassion for the disadvantaged and marginalized, but we will also need to utilize the gifts cities have to offer as they shape world culture and make the gospel accessible in every community, town, or village.

The city of Portland, its Christian organizations, and civic agencies—along with other cities mentioned in these pages—have, hopefully, provided the reader with a glimpse of how great God's love is for people and places. God is good and he is always at work . . . everywhere. As people continue to look to the city for shelter, services, professional collaboration, artistic endeavors, and a sense of community, Christ-followers will be there. A new generation of Christians are returning to the city—a generation willing to address their biases, human and theological!

The return to concentrated population centers around the globe will no doubt bring a change to status quo ministry methods. The words of a wise elder in my organization have stayed with me as a steady reminder of what is ahead. The frail, wheelchair-bound woman with a prophetic edge, proclaimed the next generation would lead with "creativity and courage" and become a "contrast and a consolation to the world."

Bringing a foretaste of God's kingdom *now*, will require courage and creativity. With boldness, city pastors and practitioners will encounter diversity of people and ideas daily; and they will find the masterful presentation of the gospel—in word and deed—to be essential in the grit and glamour of our cities. The need to bravely address uncomfortable city issues—such as racism, poverty, homelessness or human trafficking—will find us at odds with the religious and non-religious alike. The need to creatively utilize space, incorporate business with the mission of God, or incarnationally live among the people we are called to reach, will raise eyebrows in some sectors. The questions will come and we will need to stand firm on the Truth of Scripture, confident in his hope for the city.

The reservations of some, rather than cause conflict or discord, can be met with the contrast of Christlikeness—a life and ministry filled with kindness and compassion. A friend recently remarked that a relative had accused him of being "too compassionate." Our reality, at this moment in history, is a world that is often harsh with hatred, indifference, and criticism. The church, all Christ-followers, have everything we need to be a people of contrast—*too* much compassion is the optimal goal!

Our surrender to God in an urban world will be risky. Some of us will find the risk to be foremost an internal struggle. Others will experience external threats or challenges. Most of us will deal with both. In the midst of our personal journey, we will corporately experience his solutions. There is community joy when "all things come together in Christ." Our hearts will be, at last, made whole as we discover that God has indeed made us to love him and to love our neighbor. May the Holy Spirit amply supply his power to bravely risk the road ahead. May we value every city and the unique story

God is telling through its places and people. And . . . may we never forget that the God of the universe has invited us, through his Son, to be *in* and *of* the Kingdom story he's authored.

Thank you for bearing with me as I recorded my journey and those of a handful of urban practitioners. Where my story or the stories of others may have been incomplete or unclear, I pray the Spirit of Christ Jesus would make your story and pathway distinctively well-defined and his "road-tested" direction "straight and smooth."

A Final Word

The closing chapters of this book were penned in the spring and early summer of 2020. During this period, the U.S. joined the ranks of nations affected by the global pandemic known as COVID19. The virus has, so far, claimed over four hundred thousand lives worldwide,[171] created economic hardships, and initiated unprecedented social isolation. Disproportionately affected were the poor, minorities, and the elderly. Immigration came to a stunning halt and refugees were held in place until further notice—some forced to remain in camps riddled with COVID. Amid the chaos, pain, and devastation of such widespread suffering, America was forced to face another out-of-control virus infecting the soul of our nation.

The death of George Floyd, a black man brutally murdered by police, sparked protests in numerous American cities. The injustice reached a boiling point as Floyd was added to a long list of black citizens killed by law enforcement. As with so many peaceful demonstrations, instigators (often those uninterested in the reason for protest) engaged in violence, creating yet another distraction from the ceaseless cry of the African American community. Systemic racism isn't new, but often veiled. Much like the biological virus, COVID19, prejudice spreads from asymptomatic carriers as well as those who are blatantly sick, and the effects are evident.

---

[171] CNN Health, "The U.S. Has 4% of the World's Population but 25% of Its Corona Virus Cases," 2020, accessed June 15, 2020.

These two recent events have had a profound impact on major cities. The world has stood helplessly by as crowded urban neighborhoods isolated their citizens in hopes of curtailing the spread of a highly contagious virus. The scientific and medical community has been challenged with an over-abundance of patients and a lack of any real treatment. The creation of a vaccine is hopeful, but takes significant time to develop. The impact has been tangibly unsettling in a myriad of intangible ways—we simply don't have control.

Likewise, racism is out-of-control. It is harbored both in the heart of humankind and in systems. Government leaders and church leaders have looked the other way far too long. Focused on prosperity, we have lost our sense of justice. From the top down, we've compromised God's value for human life. Of King Zedekiah, the Bible speaks, "He was set in his own stubborn ways—he never gave God a thought; repentance never entered his mind. The evil mindset spread to the leaders and priests and filtered down to the people—it kicked off an epidemic of evil . . . (II Chr 36:13-14 The Message)." Racism, plain and simple, is an epidemic of evil.

The widespread injustice can never be blamed entirely on those in authority. Each of us must come to a place of awareness, repentance, and action. I have had to deal with my own heart, allowing God to examine the ways I so easily "categorize" whole people groups due to color, socio-economic standing, or even profession. There is an ongoing question of how I can participate in the healing—not with insincere platitudes or trite answers, but with a willingness to connect my life to the lives of those who are suffering at this moment. For me, and for so many of us, prayers of repentance and prayers for God to direct future action will keep us firmly on our knees in the days to come.

The profound effect of these current events can lead to hopelessness based in lack of control, fear, disillusionment, or simply the thought that nothing will ever change. As urban dwellers once again leave the city—this time due to sickness or violence, its time a new breed of urban missionaries and practitioners rise to the occasion. The CITY is, by God's design, full of goodness. The people who inhabit those cities have a STORY—and we need to listen like never before. The city, wherever we live, is about all of US—*we are in this together.*

That phrase—"We are in this together"—has been repeatedly uttered during the COVID19 quarantine. Another collective phrase, "Black lives matter," has been shouted with passion throughout the land. Will we *finally* believe they do? Will we at last believe that the seemingly endless virus of racism can be cured if we are willing to resist the evil in our hearts, put our hope in the God of justice, and risk surrender to Christ's ways?

The "viruses" that have come to light in recent weeks must not become the end of the story, but rather a new start to live out the love of Christ in ways that transform hearts, lead to the transformation of our institutions and systems, and prepare people and places for his return. Neither COVID 19 nor racism can deter God's intended work in an individual, a city, or a nation. The story, in many ways, is at a Book of Acts crossroad. As disciples, we can wish for the days when things were better *or* we can seize the opportunity adversity brings and reach Jerusalem, Judea, and the uttermost parts of the world with the gospel. We can remain in a state of separation from our brothers and sisters in Christ, or we can leave our prejudice on the roof with Peter and go visit Cornelius. We can avoid urban centers where disease and violence may be prevalent, or we can join Paul and start churches in every major city of the known world!

May we choose the right and righteous path.

References

Administration, U.S. Economic Developement. "U.S. Economic
   Development Prioritizes Applications for Projects Located in
   Opportunity Zones." https://www.eda.gov/news/press-
   releases/2019/06/12/opportunity-zones.htm 2019. Accessed May
   12, 2020.

Barrie, L.A. "Timeimage, Reflections of Portland: Portland's Black
   Community and the Church." *The Neighborhood History Project,
   Bureau of Parks and Recreation* 1, no. 2 (1979): 36.

Belles, Nita. "In Our Backyard : Human Trafficking in America and What
   We Can Do to Stop It." 2015.

Benesh, Sean. *The Urbanity of the Bible*. Portland, OR: Urban Loft
   Publishers, 2015.

Benesh, Sean. *View from the Urban Loft: Developing a Framework for
   Understanding the City*. Eugene, OR: Resource Publications, 2011.

Beshore, Laurie. *Love without Walls : Learning to Be a Church in the World
   for the World*. Grand Rapids, MI: Zondervan, 2012.

Brisco, Thomas V. *Holman Bible Atlas*. Nashville, TN: Broadman & Holman,
   1998.

Bureau, U.S. Census. "2017 Poverty Statistics." 2017. Accessed April 15,
   2019. https://www.census.gov/search-
   results.html?q=percentage+of+US+citizens+living+under+the+pov
   erty+level&page=1&stateGeo=none&searchtype=web&cssp=SERP&
   charset=UTF-8.

Business Insider, James Pasley. "20 Staggering Facts About Human
   Trafficking in the U.S." https://www.businessinsider.com/human-
   trafficking-in-the-us-facts-statistics-2019-7. 2019. Accessed May 4,
   2020.

Center, Human Trafficking. "The Profits Made from Human Trafficking."
   Accessed May 4, 2020.

Center, Refugee Processing. "Admissions and Arrivals, Admissions Report 2020." https://www.wrapsnet.org/admissions-and-arrivals/ 2020. Accessed June 10, 2020.

Center, Salem Dream. "A Walk on the Edge." http://salemdreamcenter.org. Accessed March 20, 2020.

Comer, John Mark. *Garden City: Work, Rest, and the Art of Being Human.* Grand Rapids, MI: Zondervan, 2015.

Congress, Library of. "Contributor Biographical Information for Cities." http://catdir.loc.gov/catdir/enhancements/fy0628/2005440738-b.html. 2004. Accessed March 10, 2016.

Conn, Harvie M., and Manuel Ortiz. *Urban Ministry : The Kingdom, the City, & the People of God.* Downers Grove, Ill.: InterVarsity Press, 2001.

Corbett, Steve, and Brian Fikkert. *When Helping Hurts : How to Alleviate Poverty without Hurting the Poor-- and Yourself.* Chicago, IL: Moody Publishers, 2009.

Corey Pein, Willamette Week. "The Other Portland." http://www.wweek.com/portland/article-18071-the-other-portland.html. 2017. Accessed Jan 31, 2017.

Corporation, Rockwood Community Development. "Rockwood Cdc 2015 Annual Report." https://www.rockwoodcdc.org/wp-content/uploads/2016/01/Rockwood-CDC-Annual-Report-2015.pdf. 2016. Accessed April 5, 2016.

Crane, Linda Bergquist and Michael D. *City Shaped Churches, Planting Churches in a Global Era.* Skyforest, CA: Urban Loft, 2018.

Department, U.S. State. "2019 Trafficking in Persons Report." https://www.state.gov/reports/2019-trafficking-in-persons-report/. 2019. Accessed May 4, 2020.

Dictionary, Urban. "First World Problems." Urban Dictionary. Accessed November 6, 2018.

Elliott, Barbara J. *Street Saints : Renewing America's Cities*. Philadelphia: Templeton Foundation Press, 2004.

Encyclopedia, The Oregon. "Denorval Unthank." https://oregonencyclopedia.org/articles/unthank_denorval_1899_1977 . Accessed April 30, 2017.

Foundation, Annie E. Casey. "What Is Foster Care, Updated April 14, 2020." https://www.aecf.org/topics/foster-care/ 2020. Accessed April 30, 2020.

Foundation Kids Count Data Center, Annie E. Casey Foundtion. "Children in Poverty by Race and Ethnicity." https://datacenter.kidscount.org/data/tables/44-children-in-poverty-by-race-and-ethnicity#detailed/1/any/false/. 2018. Accessed April 25, 2019.

Gesenius, Wilhelm, James Strong, and Samuel Prideaux Tregelles. *Gesenius' Hebrew and Chaldee Lexicon to the Old Testament Scriptures : Numerically Coded to Strong's Exhaustive Concordance, with an English Index of More Than 12,000 Entries*. Grand Rapids: Baker Book House, 1979.

González, Justo L. *The Story of Christianity. Volume 1, the Early Church to the Reformation*. Rev. and updated [ed.], 2nd ed. New York: HarperCollins, 2010.

Gornik, Mark R. *To Live in Peace : Biblical Faith and the Changing Inner City*. Grand Rapids, Mich.: W.B. Eerdmans Pub., 2002.

Gornik, Mark R. *To Live in Peace: Biblical Faith and the Changing Inner City*. Grand Rapids, MI: W.B. Eerdmans Pub., 2002.

Grimm, Carl Ludwig Wilibald, Christian Gottlob Wilke, Joseph Henry Thayer, and James Strong. *A Greek-English Lexicon of the New Testament : Being Grimm's Wilke's Clavis Novi Testamenti*. Grand Rapids: Baker Book House, 1977.

Health, CNN. "The U.S. Has 4% of the World's Population but 25% of Its Corona Virus Cases." 2020. Accessed June 15, 2020.

Henry, Matthew. *Matthew Henry's Commentary on the Whole Bible*. Vol.
Volume 6, Acts to Revelation. Peabody, MA: Hendrickson
Publishers, 1991.

Heuertz, Christopher L., and Christine D. Pohl. *Friendship at the Margins :
Discovering Mutuality in Service and Mission. Resources for
Reconciliation*. Downers Grove, IL: IVP Books, 2010.

Hoang, Bethany H. *The Justice Calling : Where Passion Meets
Perseverance*.

Homelessness, National Alliance to End. "Homelessness in America."
Accessed April 25, 2019.
https://endhomelessness.org/homelessness-in-
america/homelessness-statistics/state-of-homelessness-report/.

Interpreter Magazine, "Means of Grace-Offering Mercy, Receiving Grace".
"Http://Www.Interpretermagazine.Org/Topics/Means-of-Grace-
Offering-Mercy-Receiving-Grace#Main." Accessed March 28, 2017.

Keener, Craig S., and InterVarsity Press. *The Ivp Bible Background
Commentary : New Testament*. Downers Grove, Ill.: InterVarsity
Press, 1993.

Keller, Tim. "What Is Biblical Justice."
http://www.relevantmagazine.com/god/practical-faith/what-
biblical-justice. 2012. Accessed February 12, 2013.

Keller, Timothy. *Why God Made Cities*. New York: Redeemer City to City,
2013.

Kelly, Brandon. "Future Church: 10 Predictions for the Next 10 Years." 2018.
Accessed Nov 3, 2018.

Kevin Palau. (Interview by author, Portland, OR, October 18, 2011.

Kysar, Robert. *Called to Care : Biblical Images for Social Ministry*.
Minneapolis: Fortress Press, 1991.

Kysar, Robert. *Called to Care: Biblical Images for Social Ministry*.
Minneapolis: Fortress Press, 1991.

Lausanne Congress. "The Manila Manifesto."
https://www.lausanne.org/content/manifesto/the-manila-
manifesto. 1989. Accessed August 28, 2017.

Levison, John R. *40 Days with the Holy Spirit : Fresh Air for Every Day.*
Brewster, MA: Paraclete Press, 2015.

Morgan, G. Campbell. *Studies in the Four Gospels: The Gospel of Luke.* Old
Tappan, N.J.: Fleming H. Revell Company, 1931.

Morgan, G. Campbell. *Studies in the Four Gospels: The Gospel of Matthew.*
Old Tappan, N.J.: Fleming H. Revell Company, 1931.

Nations, United. "The World's Cities in 2016."
http://www.un.org/en/development/desa/population/publications
/pdf/urbanization/the_worlds_cities_in_2016_data_booklet.pdf.
2016. Accessed (March 10, 2016).

New Advent, Catholic Encyclopedia, Acts of Corporal and Spiritual Mercy.
"Http://Www.Newadvent.Org/Cathen/10198d.Htm." Accessed
March 29, 2017.

New York Times, Rikha Sharma Rani. "Homes to Heal Trafficked Children."
https://www.nytimes.com/2019/06/19/opinion/foster-child-
trafficking.html 2019. Accessed June 1, 2020.

Newbigin, Lesslie. *The Gospel in a Pluralist Society.* Grand Rapids,
Mich.,Geneva SZ: W.B. Eerdmans ; WCC Publications, 1989.

News, BBC. "Syria Conflict: Aleppo Bombarded as Un Warns of Bleak
Moment." http://www.bbc.com/news/world-middle-east-
38023368. 2016. Accessed November 18, 2016.

Now, End Slavery. "Human Trafficking, Refugees and Displaced Persons:
What Terms to Use "
http://www.endslaverynow.org/blog/articles/human-trafficking-
refugees-and-displaced-persons-what-terms-to-use. 2015. Accessed
June 15, 2020.

NYC, Dream Center. http://www.dreamcenter.nyc. Accessed March 20,
2020.

Oregon, Community Development Corporation of. "2019 Annual Report." https://www.rockwoodcdc.org/wp-content/uploads/2020/02/CDCO-2019-Annual-Report.pdf). 2020. Accessed May 13, 2020.

OregonLive. "Most of Oregon'a Homeless Live on Street, in Cars, Parks: Highest Percentage in U.S., Says Hud Report, Http://Www.Oregonlive.Com/Trending/2016/11/Homeless_Unsheltered_Oregon_Hu.Html." 2016. Accessed February 28, 2017.

OregonLive. "North Portland's Untahnk Park Is Rededicated." 2011. Accessed May 1, 2017.

Pastor, Paul J. *The Face of the Deep: Exploring the Mysterious Person of the Holy Spirit*. Colorado Springs, CO: David C. Cook, 2016.

Pew Research, Drew Desilver. "U.S. Public Seldom Has Welcomed Refugees into Country." https://www.pewresearch.org/fact-tank/2015/11/19/u-s-public-seldom-has-welcomed-refugees-into-country/ 2015. Accessed March 10, 2020.

Pintarich, Dick, ed., *The Struggle of Blacks in Oregon. Great and Minor Moments in Oregon's History*. edited by Dick Pintarich. Portland: New Oregon Publishers, Inc., 2008.

Plan, Empowerment. https://www.empowermentplan.org/about) 2020. Accessed May 1, 2020.

Rah, Soong-Chan. *The Next Evangelicalism : Releasing the Church from Western Cultural Captivity*. Downers Grove, Ill.: IVP Books, 2009.

Reader, John. *Cities*. New York, NY: Grove Press, 2004.

Research, Lifeway. "Evangelical View on Immigration Report." http://lifewayresearch.com/wp-content/uploads/2015/03/Evangelical-Views-on-Immigration-Report.pdf 2015. Accessed April 10, 2020.

Robertson, A. T. *Word Pictures in the New Testament*. New York,: R. R. Smith, inc., 1930.

Ruthruff, Ron. *Closer to the Edge: Walking with Jesus for the World's Sake*. Birmingham, Alabama: New Hope Publishers, 2015.

Sayers, Mark. *Strange Days : Life in the Spirit in a Time of Upheaval*. Chicago, IL: Moody Publishers, 2017.

SCRIPTS. "Concussion." https://www.scripts.com/script-pdf/304. 2016. Accessed (December 4, 2016).

Seamands, Stephen A. *Ministry in the Image of God : The Trinitarian Shape of Christian Service*. Downers Grove, Ill.: InterVarsity Press, 2005.

Self Enhancement, Inc. "This Is Our Story." https://www.selfenhancement.org/history. Accessed April 30, 2017.

Seremet, Beth. "Leading Your Congregation to Welcome the Stranger in a Politically Complex Environment." 2020.

Sherman, Amy L. *Kingdom Calling : Vocational Stewardship for the Common Good*. Downers Grove, IL: IVP Books, 2011.

Sider, Ronald J., Philip N. Olson, and Heidi Rolland Unruh. *Churches That Make a Difference : Reaching Your Community with Good News and Good Works*. Grand Rapids, Mich.: Baker Books, 2002.

Smith, Colin. *Mind the Gap: Reflections from Luke's Gospel on the Divided City*. Portland, OR: Urban Loft Publishers, 2015.

Snyder, Howard A. *Small Voice, Big City: The Challenge of Urban Mission*. Skyforest, CA: Urban Loft Publishers, 2016.

Spees, Randy White and H. *Out of Nazareth: Christ-Centered Civic Transformation*. Skyforest, CA: Urban Loft, 2017.

Stark, Rodney. *The Rise of Christianity: A Sociologist Reconciles History*. Princeton, N.J.: Princeton University Press, 1996.

Statista, Erin Duffin. "Syrian Refugee Arrival in the United States from 2011-2019." https://www.statista.com/statistics/742553/syrian-refugee-arrivals-us/) 2020. Accessed March 10, 2020.

The Lausanne Congress. "The Lausanne Covenant." http://www.lausanne.org/content/covenant/lausanne-covenant. 1974. Accessed August 27, 2017.

The New York Times. "South Carolina Cold Case Killer."
http://www.nytimes.com/aponline/2016/11/11/us/ap-us-south-
carolina-cold-case-killer.html?_r=0. 2016. Accessed November 14,
2016.

Tribune, The Chicago. "Teen in Utah School Sabbings of Five Classmates
Booked on Attempted Murder."
http://www.chicagotribune.com/news/nationworld/ct-utah-high-
school-stabbing-201story.html. 2016. Accessed November 14, 2016.

U.S. Department of Health and Human Services, Office of Inspector
General. "State's Prevention of Child Sex Trafficking in Foster Care."
https://www.oig.hhs.gov/reports-and-
publications/workplan/summary/wp-summary-0000396.asp.
2019. Accessed June 15, 2020.

VanDyke, Kris Rock and Joel. *Geography of Grace: Doing Theology from
Below*. United States: Center for Transforming Mission, 2012.

Voyager, Boston. "Meet Sheila Donegan of Boston Dream Center Downtown
Boston." http://bostonvoyager.com/interview/meet-sheila-
donegan-boston-dream-center-downtown-boston-heart-city/. 2018.
Accessed September 12, 2018.

Waltke, Bruce K. *The Book of Proverbs*. 2 vols. *The New International
Commentary on the Old Testament*. Grand Rapids, Mich.: William
B. Eerdmans Pub., 2004.

Wayne, Lil. "How to Love." Tha Carter IV.
https://www.bing.com/videos/search?q=how+to+love+lil+wayne&
view=detail&mid=3225073A1AC37FCE34123225073A1AC37FCE34
12&FORM=VIRE0&ru=%2fsearch%3fq%3dhow%2bto%2blove%2bl
il%2bwayne%26form%3dAPMCS1%26PC%3dAPMC, . Accessed
April 15, 2020.

Week, Willamette. "Portland Is Still the Strip Club Capital of America,
http://Www.Wweek.Com/Portland/Blog-33364-Portland-Is-Still-

the-Strip-Club-Capital-of-America.Html." 2015. Accessed February 28, 2017.

Werking, Natalie. *Reaching Kids in the Community*. Commissioned by Jesus. Washington, D.C., 2017.

White, Randy. *Encounter God in the City : Onramps to Personal and Community Transformation*. Downers Grove, Ill.: IVP Books, 2006. http://www.loc.gov/catdir/toc/ecip0612/2006013027.html.

Wikipedia. "Nicknames of Boston." https://en.wikipedia.org/wiki/Nicknames_of_Boston. Accessed April 27, 2019.

Wolterstorff, Nicholas, Clarence W. Joldersma, and Gloria Goris Stronks. *Educating for Shalom: Essays on Christian Higher Education*. Grand Rapids, MI: W.B. Eerdmans Pub. Co., 2004.

Wright, Christopher J. H. *The Mission of God : Unlocking the Bible's Grand Narrative*. Downers Grove, Ill.: IVP Academic, 2006.

Wright, N. T. *Simply Good News : Why the Gospel Is News and What Makes It Good*. FIRST EDITION. ed.

Made in the USA
Middletown, DE
06 March 2021